Avinash Dixit

MICROECONOMICS

A Very Short Introduction

OXFORD
UNIVERSITY PRESS

OXFORD
UNIVERSITY PRESS

Great Clarendon Street, Oxford, OX2 6DP,
United Kingdom

Oxford University Press is a department of the University of Oxford.
It furthers the University's objective of excellence in research, scholarship,
and education by publishing worldwide. Oxford is a registered trade mark of
Oxford University Press in the UK and in certain other countries

Published in the United States of America by Oxford University Press
198 Madison Avenue, New York, NY 10016, United States of America

British Library Cataloguing in Publication Data
Data available

Library of Congress Control Number: 2013953432

ISBN 978-0-19-968937-8

Printed in Great Britain by
Ashford Colour Press Ltd, Gosport, Hampshire

Microeconomics: A Very Short Introduction

VERY SHORT INTRODUCTIONS are for anyone wanting a stimulating and accessible way in to a new subject. They are written by experts, and have been translated into more than 40 different languages.

The Series began in 1995, and now covers a wide variety of topics in every discipline. The VSI library now contains over 350 volumes—a Very Short Introduction to everything from Psychology and Philosophy of Science to American History and Relativity—and continues to grow in every subject area.

Very Short Introductions available now:

Available soon:

For more information visit our website
www.oup.com/vsi/

Contents

Preface

Non-economists think economics is about unemployment, inflation, growth, competitiveness of nations, and other matters pertaining to the economy as a whole, or in economists' jargon, about *macroeconomics*. They rarely mention, and perhaps are not even aware of, the whole nexus of choices and transactions behind the larger picture: people's choices of where to live and work, how much to save, what to buy, and so on; firms' decisions about location, investment, hiring, firing, advertising, and many other dimensions of business; and government policies with regard to infrastructure, regulation of industries, structure and rates of taxes on goods and services, and so on. Citizens' relative ignorance and neglect of these fine-level, or *microeconomic*, issues is partly explained by the fact that things often work pretty well at that level, and when they don't work so well, each failure seems small in the larger scheme of things. But many such small failures can add up to a large economic cost. They can have large ramifications at the macroeconomic level too. Therefore it is important to understand why things work pretty well in the microeconomy much of the time, when and why they fail in little and big ways, and what to do to guard against and cope with such failures. In this book, I attempt to present this way of thinking about economics, and some of the conclusions it yields. I hope to convince non-specialist readers that microeconomics is important, and connects as closely with their daily life as unemployment and inflation. I hope to give them some aha moments, where they say, 'I have often seen this; now I understand why!' For more lasting value, I hope to equip them with some basic concepts and tools of microeconomic analysis for use in their own thinking and actions, and leave them eager to do the further reading that I recommend.

Three caveats before you begin. First, in this *Very Short Introduction* you should not look for anything like a comprehensive treatment of the subject. I had to leave out many topics, ideas, and methods, not because they are unimportant, but because in my opinion others have a stronger claim in a brief introduction. If you are a microeconomist and your favourite topic is missing, blame my tastes.

Second, economics has an unavoidable quantitative aspect that requires a little numeracy, for example reading tables and graphs. I have kept these topics as simple as I could, but readers who have occasional trouble with the graphs or numbers can usually just skip those parts and read the rest.

Third, while I hope the subject is fascinating and my treatment readable, such a book cannot be a page-turner. If you are new to the subject, do not try to read too much at one go. Stealing from P. G. Wodehouse's preface to his collected Jeeves short stories, I advise: Do not attempt to finish this volume at one sitting. It can be done—I did it myself when correcting the proofs—but it leaves one weak and is really not worth doing just for the sake of saying you have done it. Take it easy. Spread it out. Assimilate it little by little. Take one small section with each meal. Should insomnia strike, add another section or two at night.

Drafts of a book intended for intelligent non-economist readers should be tried out on intelligent non-economists. I am fortunate to have just the right friends: my breakfast group at Small World

Coffee. I am very grateful to Frank Calaprice (physicist), Julie Jetton (lawyer), Bill Shaffer (financial adviser), Connie Shaffer (high-school French teacher), and Cathy Smith (hypnotherapist) for their patience and generosity in reading early drafts and telling me what needed clarification, rewriting, or even deletion. Andrea Keegan at Oxford University Press and her colleagues also provided valuable feedback on matters of style as well as substance.

Fellow economists were also generous with their time and advice, correcting my errors and suggesting better examples and explanations. Karla Hoff has my eternal gratitude for combining this role with that of an eagle-eyed copy-editor. I am also very grateful to Dilip Abreu, Paul Klemperer and John Vickers for their perceptive comments and useful suggestions.

My biggest *Thank You* goes to all the teachers, colleagues, and students from whom I have absorbed and improved understanding of microeconomics over my whole career. Much of what is good in the book is your doing; the defects are mine.

List of illustrations

List of tables

Chapter 1
What and why of microeconomics

A wake-up call

Every morning I choose among several alternatives for my jolt of caffeine. I can brew coffee at home, go to a national chain coffee shop like Starbucks, or to go to Princeton's local Small World Coffee. If I choose to go out, I can walk, bike, or drive. With my coffee I can have healthy bran and berries, indulge in a muffin full of carbs and fat, or binge on fats and salt with eggs and bacon.

What I choose depends on many considerations: whether it is raining or snowing, whether I overindulged at dinner the night before and need exercise, whether my friends have congregated and I feel like socializing that morning, sheer whim or desire for variety, and the quality and prices of the coffee and eats at the different places (including the value of my time if I make coffee at home). As these conditions change from day to day or month to month, my choices also change. But never have I arrived at a coffee shop only to be told, 'Sorry; we don't have any coffee today'. Nor has the supermarket ever run out of coffee when I went to buy some to brew at home. How did they know I would come, and why were they ready and willing to serve me? Examining my choices one step back, when I went to buy a car that (among other trips) I would drive to the coffee shop or the supermarket, how did someone anticipate my demand and have the car available?

Microeconomics studies how millions of consumers choose what goods and services to buy, how producers make decisions to meet these demands, and how the two sides interact. Much of the time the transactions work fairly smoothly. That is why microeconomics is often a story of the dog that did not bark in the night, which in turn explains why non-economists are often unaware of any microeconomic problems. But from time to time things do go wrong. At a trivial level, the coffee shop does run out of muffins on a few days when I am late (although I can then get a scone or some other carb fix instead). But some failures are more drastic, like the gasoline shortages in the 1970s and the housing bubble and its collapse in the 2000s. Therefore it behooves all intelligent people to get some basic understanding of microeconomics: when and how transactions go well, when and why they fail, and what can be done when they do fail or threaten to fail.

Information and incentives

In most societies, consumers and producers interact in markets— not necessarily traditional bazaars and marketplaces, but shops, restaurants, other venues like bargaining tables and auctions, and increasingly the internet. In a market, buyers pay a price to sellers for the good or service. This price serves a twofold purpose. First, if something is scarce, its price rises; thus a high price conveys *information* about scarcity. Second, when a price is high, a supplier of that good or service can profit by producing more of it, and buyers will buy less or switch to something else; thus a high price also provides a natural *incentive* for actions that alleviate the scarcity. Information and incentive mechanisms to coordinate transactions between producers and consumers, and specifically whether and how prices work in this dual capacity, are the main subject matter of microeconomics.

The focus on information and incentives also tells us when and why the price mechanism can fail: it may convey inadequate or wrong information or incentives, or responses to these signals may not occur. The most frequent failure of this kind arises when one person's actions have spillover effects on others. Every car driver contributes to air pollution, which increases the scarcity of clean air. But there is no market or price for clean air, so no one gets a signal of that scarcity and no one has a profit incentive to alleviate it.

The price mechanism can also fail if responses to its signals are suppressed. Price controls suppress them. So do barriers to entry of new producers: whether natural barriers, strategic ones erected by entrenched producers, or those created by government policies. Further, existing producers can conspire to preserve some scarcity so as to drive up the price for their own greater profit. In socialist countries where production and supply are in the hands of the state, its functionaries have little to gain personally by satisfying consumers and suffer few penalties by neglecting them. Without markets the functionaries even lack good information about scarcity. That is why those systems have chronic shortages and poor quality.

More subtly, the price mechanism may fail by conveying information about matters besides scarcity. Suppose you know that used 2010 Toyota Camrys are listed for around $15,000, but don't know the quality of the particular car you are contemplating buying. You infer that the car cannot be worth much more than $15,000—otherwise the previous owner, who has had plenty of opportunity to observe its quality, wouldn't be selling it. But it could be worth less—much less. That depresses your willingness to pay. When all buyers think this and hold back, the lower demand leads to a lower price, driving even more owner-sellers out of the market. In the worst-case scenario, the whole market can collapse. Of course sellers of good cars and buyers who want good cars can both benefit by enabling credible communication of information about quality. The signals they use for this purpose are also subjects for microeconomic analysis.

A different kind of market failure arises from a moral or ethical perspective. The signals and incentives of the price mechanism are ineffective if would-be buyers don't have the purchasing power to back up their desire. The Pieman said to Simple Simon: 'Show me first your penny,' and Simon had to reply: 'Indeed I have not any'. This is a trivial example, but we may legitimately regard some wants such as health and education as meritorious or basic human rights, regardless of a person's private ability to pay for them. Deciding and implementing policies to fulfill such wants become an issue in political economy.

Prices and payments don't have to be in conventional money. One thing may be exchanged for another; payment may be deferred either as a loan or as a general favour owed. Depending on the context, one form of 'currency' may be more appropriate and effective than another. Money is crass and inappropriate in many social situations; informal arrangements of reciprocity and favour exchanges prevail among families and friends. Elaborate algorithms and organizations have evolved for matching hospitals and freshly graduated doctors, and for multilateral exchanges of organs, for example kidneys, when most people would regard their sale for money as abhorrent. Interpreted broadly and adapted to fit the context, economic analysis can be applied with considerable success to all these many and varied interactions and transactions.

So much to tell, so little space! Therefore, enough introductory chat and motivation—let us begin with the end-users of economic activity, namely consumers.

Chapter 2
Consumers

Substitution

Consumers make their decisions using some combination of calculation and instinct, and taking into account many aspects, of which the price of what they are considering buying is only one. Microeconomics pays attention to other aspects too, but focuses on prices to study the interaction of each consumer with the rest of the economy. A very broadly valid property of consumer choice, almost general enough to merit the name *law of demand* that is sometimes attached to it, is that when the price of something rises, other things being equal, less of it will be purchased.

The main explanation for this empirical regularity is *substitution*. Consumers respond to a price increase by buying less of that commodity, instead they satisfy their desires, perhaps imperfectly so, by substituting it with something else relatively cheaper. As an example, suppose the price of lager rises while that of ale stays unchanged. Consider a consumer who chose lager at the original prices. At the new prices the preference for lager is to some extent outweighed by its increased cost, so the consumer may settle for drinking less lager and more ale, that is, he or she may substitute ale for lager. If the preference for lager is not very strong, or if the price rise is very large, the consumer may switch completely to ale.

Elementary textbooks illustrate substitution using a few commodity groups (aggregates) such as food and clothing. Readers may rightly wonder how one can substitute clothing for food. If the price of food rises, can wearing more clothes on a cold day to reduce the loss of body heat adequately make up for eating less? In reality the choice is not between broad commodity groups. Instead it is between subcategories such as chicken and fish, or cotton and wool—and the narrower the categories, the greater the possibility of substitution. Actually, a little substitution occurs even at the level of broad categories, as we will soon see in an example of statistical estimation of demand.

Ability to substitute depends on time scale. A consumer with fixed habits will need time to change the mindset or cultivate taste for the substitute commodity. A coffee addict will not switch to tea unless the price of coffee rises by a lot and for a long time. The owner of a house heated by an oil-burning furnace, seeing the price of natural gas fall, may not switch to a gas furnace until the old furnace breaks down. If a price increase is expected to be temporary, the consumer may choose to ride out the increase; many consumers literally do so in their fuel-guzzler cars when the price of the fuel rises.

The relationship between the price of something and its quantity demanded is useful for economic analysis only if it is reasonably stable and can be estimated or forecast. Any one person's demand is influenced by many idiosyncratic chance factors. Luckily for the study of markets, we need only know the total or aggregate response of consumers. This makes the market demand more stable and predictable.

Aggregating demand over consumers has two effects. First, the random part of individual consumers' decisions, whether due to whim or to some idiosyncratic change in circumstances, gets averaged out to zero by the law of large numbers. Second, one consumer's substitution may be sudden, shifting from buying one type of car to another, or from car-driving to bike-riding; this gets smoothed out because different consumers shift at different prices and each of them is only a tiny part of the market. Therefore overall market demand becomes a smoother and more stable relationship than that for an individual.

The quantity of any one commodity that is demanded in the market depends not only on its own price but also on other factors. This is not a problem as long as these can be estimated and predicted. Some factors affect the market as a whole, such as advertising and seasons of the year. Most important for market analysis are prices of other related commodities. For example, if the price of lager increases, consumers will substitute it with ale; therefore at any given price of ale, more of it will be demanded than before.

Complements

However, suppose most consumers eat fish and chips together. If the price of fish increases (while that of chips stays unchanged), this increases the price of the fish-and-chips combo, so less of it is bought. Therefore for any given price of chips, their quantity demanded decreases when the price of fish rises. Consumers do not substitute away from fish toward chips: the two commodities are not substitutes for each other, but *complements*. This distinction proves important for organization of markets for such pairs, as we will see in Chapter 5 when we examine profit externalities among firms.

Demand curves

The relationship between the price of a good and its quantity demanded is best illustrated graphically. For readers unfamiliar with this representation of a relationship between two entities, here is a brief explanation (see Figure 1). The vertical and horizontal lines are called 'axes'. In our context the vertical line is

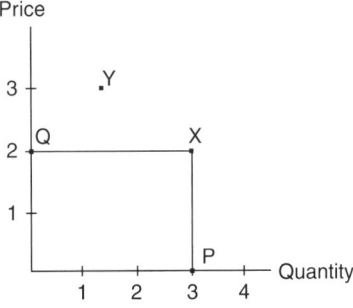

1. Representation of a point

the price axis, and the horizontal line the quantity axis. Any point in the area enclosed by the two axes represents a price–quantity combination. In Figure 1, from any point such as the one labelled X, look at the lines parallel to the two axes: XP parallel to the price axis and XQ parallel to the quantity axis. Then X represents a combination of price equal to the length XP and quantity equal to the length XQ. Thus in the figure, X represents price = 2 (dollars per bottle of lager, say) and quantity = 3 (million bottles of lager).

To reinforce your understanding, draw similar parallel lines from the point labelled Y and check that it represents the combination price = 3, quantity = 1.5. For more details, see <http://www.mathopenref.com/tocs/coordpointstoc.html>.

Figure 2 uses this method to show how the price of a good influences the total demand for it. This is called a (market) *demand curve*; it is best thought of as a sum of many different individuals' choices at each price. Suppose the good in question is the one in our opening example—namely, lager. The upper left hand portion of the curve, where the price is high and quantity small, comes from those few people with the strongest preference for lager who are willing to pay the highest prices. At lower prices

Microeconomics

8

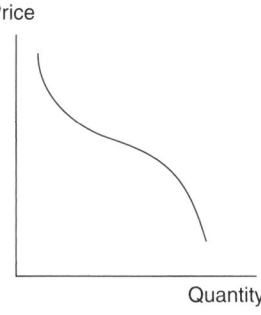

Price

Quantity

2. A market demand curve

of lager, the quantity demanded increases as the lager-lovers drink even more, and more importantly, as ale-drinkers and some wine-drinkers substitute away from those into the now-cheaper lager. Finally, at very low prices, perhaps even some tea-drinkers may try lager.

As new consumers enter the picture at successively lower prices, the added quantities are actually horizontal lines in the graph and the demand curve consists of steps. But there are thousands or millions of consumers, so each step is tiny in relation to the whole market, and the demand curve looks smooth to a sufficient degree of accuracy.

The market demand curve shows the relationship between the quantity demanded of something and its own price. This relationship changes when some third thing in the background— the price of a substitute or complement, or consumers' incomes— changes. Figure 3 shows such a shift. Suppose the demand curve is for coffee. When the price of tea (a substitute) rises, the quantity of coffee demanded increases for any given price of coffee; the demand curve for coffee shifts to the right. A similar shift to the right occurs if consumers' incomes increase. Or suppose the figure shows the demand curve for fish; it shifts to the right when the price of chips (a complement) falls.

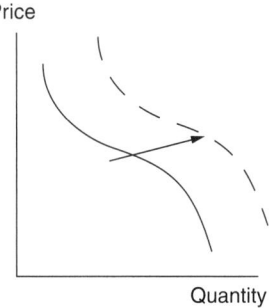

Price

Quantity

3. Shift of the demand curve

To understand the effects of changes such as taxes or technical progress, as we will do later, we will need to know the price-responsiveness of market demand. Figure 4 shows two possibilities: high responsiveness (the technical term in the jargon of economics is *elastic* demand) on the left, and low responsiveness (*inelastic* demand) on the right. Demand is likely to be more responsive if (i) good substitutes for the commodity in question are available, (ii) the time span is sufficiently long that consumers can adjust their habits or acquire

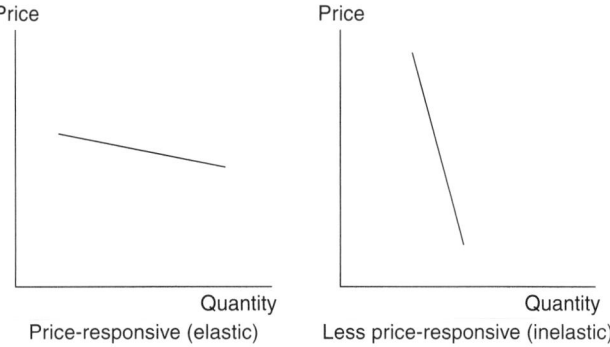

Price

Quantity
Price-responsive (elastic)

Price

Quantity
Less price-responsive (inelastic)

4. More and less price-responsive market demand curves

new tastes, or (iii) the price decrease is expected to be temporary so consumers seize the opportunity to buy. I drew these demand curves as straight lines only to bring out the concept of responsiveness in the simplest way—in reality, responsiveness can vary along the length of the demand curve, as in Figures 2 and 3.

Consumers as workers and savers

Excepting the few who live off inherited wealth, most of us earn the income that we spend as consumers. We also spread out consumption over our lifetimes, perhaps borrowing for education or home purchase in our youth, saving during our peak earning years, and winding down our savings after retirement. These decisions are amenable to analysis similar to that of demand for lager or coffee. An increase in the wage rate creates an increase in the incentive to work, substituting away from leisure; and an increase in the rate of return to savings increases the incentive to save, substituting away from immediate consumption in favour of future consumption.

However, another effect of price changes becomes important in these contexts. If your wage rate increases from $20 an hour to $25 an hour, you will probably increase your hours of work somewhat, say from 40 hours a week to 45 (to the extent that you have such flexibility). However, if your wage rate increases to $1 million per hour (you can always dream), you may choose to work for just a few hours each year: at that huge wage rate, your potential income is so large that you may choose to enjoy more leisure. This is called the *income effect* of the change in the price of your labour services. Similarly, if the rate of return to savings becomes very high, you are much wealthier, and may choose to use more of this wealth for immediate consumption, thus saving less.

Any price change has an income effect, but for commodities you buy, it normally only reinforces the substitution effect. For example, an increase in the price of meat, holding your income constant, makes you worse off; you respond by consuming less meat (and also less of other things). Only for so-called inferior goods, of which you buy more when you are worse off, can the income effect offset the substitution effect, and those are mostly curiosa for economics exams.

Statistical estimation

Many statisticians and economists have researched the relation in actual data between consumer demands and prices, incomes, and other relevant magnitudes. The broad concepts of substitution, complementarity, and income effects stand up quite well, although more refined hypotheses, especially those based on the assumption that consumers are perfectly rational calculators of their self-interest, have less success. I illustrate the general ideas using an influential survey of research on consumer behaviour by Richard Blundell of University College, London.

This work estimated the income and price responsiveness of demand for some broad commodity groups, based on the annual United Kingdom Family Expenditure Survey of households with children for the years 1970–84. Table 1 shows the effects of a 1 per cent increase in income, or in the price of a group listed in the left hand column, on the demand for the group listed at the top of each of columns 2–7. For example, when income rises by 1 per cent the consumption of alcohol rises by 2.014 per cent, and when the price of fuel rises by 1 per cent quantity of transport demanded goes down (negative number) by 0.480 per cent.

If a 1 per cent rise in income increases the consumption of something by more than 1 per cent, then richer households will spend a greater proportion of their income on this good than poorer households; in other words, it is regarded as being a luxury. Thus, alcohol is a luxury. (Many undergraduates would

Table 1. Substitution, complementarity, and income responsiveness

Effect of 1% increase in	On demand for					
	Food	**Alcohol**	**Fuel**	**Clothing**	**Transport**	**Services**
Income	0.668	2.014	0.329	1.269	1.212	1.654
Price of						
Food	−0.246	0.032	0.110	0.066	0.021	−0.004
Alcohol	0.210	−1.869	1.043	0.080	0.999	0.218
Fuel	0.464	0.671	−0.718	0.027	−0.480	0.223
Clothing	0.231	0.042	0.023	−0.716	0.163	0.045
Transport	0.048	0.345	−0.257	0.106	−0.475	0.197
Services	−0.012	0.114	−0.181	0.034	0.298	−0.587

Source: Table 2 in Blundell, *Economic Journal*, March 1988

13

do well to remember this!) Conversely, food and fuel, for which the income-responsiveness numbers are 0.668 and 0.329, constitute a larger proportion of the expenditure of households with lower incomes; these goods are necessities.

All numbers for the effects of an increase in the price of a commodity on its own quantity are negative; this confirms the law of demand, which says that demand curves slope down. If an increase in the price of item A increases the quantity demanded of item B, the two are substitutes (a positive number in the cell); this is the case for many category pairs in this study. Observe that food and clothing are substitutes, although the effect is small. Transport and fuel are complements; when the price of one goes up, the quantity demanded of the other goes down, as shown by the negative number in those cells.

Such tables underlie demand curves like the one shown in Figure 2 and its shift shown in Figure 3. For example, the demand curve for food will show its quantity and price, with the quantity decreasing by 0.246 per cent for each 1 per cent increase in the price. An increase in income, an increase in the price of alcohol (a substitute), or a decrease in the price of services (a complement) will shift the demand curve for food to the right.

Cost-of-living indexes

Probably the most important application of the principle of substitution is to cost-of-living indexes. To illustrate this in a simple way, limit the scope to the choice of two beverages: tea and coffee. Suppose the price of each is $10 per kilogram (kg), and you use 1kg of each per month. Your total monthly cost of beverages is $20. Now suppose the price of coffee doubles. At the new prices, buying 1kg of each would cost a total of $30. But you can do better by substituting tea for coffee. At the old prices you chose 1kg of each. You could have bought 900 grams of coffee and 1,100 grams of tea, but you chose not to. At the new prices, if you give up 100 grams (g) of coffee you can buy 200 g more of tea, thus getting 900g of coffee and 1,200g of tea. Suppose you like this better than your choice of 1kg of each at the old prices. Thus the combination of 900g coffee and 1,200g tea is better for you than that of 1kg of each, which in turn is better than 900g coffee and 1,100g tea. In between the two extremes, then, there must be a mix that is just as good in your preference scale as 1kg of each. Suppose this is 900g coffee and 1,150g tea. That costs 0.9 * $20 + 1.150 * $10 = $29.50. So you need only $29.50, not $30, to leave you just as satisfied with your beverage consumption at the new prices as you were at the old ones.

Cost-of-living indexes calculate the cost of buying a given bundle of consumer goods, usually the one actually chosen at an original set of prices. In this example, your beverage cost index would go up from 20 to 30, an increase of 50 per cent. But your actual cost of obtaining the same level of satisfaction increases by only $9.50, or 47.5 per cent. The conventionally calculated index overstates the effect of the price change.

The overstatement arises because the *relative* price of tea and coffee changes. If both prices had doubled to $20 per kilo, you could substitute between them one-for-one just as you did at the old prices, and you would have no reason to do so if you had none before (although you may choose to switch from beverages to other things whose prices have not risen so much).

Huge changes in relative prices occur over time. In the last several decades, prices of goods like medical care have risen far more than those of food, and prices of many electronic goods have fallen dramatically. Many wage contracts and public retirement schemes are tied to cost-of-living indexes that neglect substitution. This overcompensates workers and retirees when relative prices change and is costly to firms and governments. The solution is frequent adjustment of the quantities in the cost calculation as substitution changes choices. For example, the increase in the cost-of-living index from 2000 to 2001 is calculated using the 2000 quantities, that from 2001 to 2002 using the 2001 quantities, and so on. The increase from 2000 to 2012 is obtained by chaining together the 12 successive annual increases. But the solution is politically difficult to implement. Senior citizens resist attempts to link pension payments to a chained index. They like the overcompensation they now receive based on the fixed-weight index, and their votes matter to politicians.

Many travel and business sites offer comparisons of the cost of living in different cities, using the quantities appropriate to one base city (usually New York). This ignores substitution responding to relative price differences. For example, it ignores substitution away from expensive beef toward excellent and cheaper fish in Japan. Therefore all the other cities look more expensive relative to be base city than they should. I am sure you have noticed this when you travel.

The economy-wide consumer price index may not be appropriate for specific groups. For example, senior citizens spend more on age- and health-related items than does the population in general. Therefore their cost-of-living adjustments should be made on an index based on these quantities, not on general population aggregates. Of course there are practical limits to how fine distinctions of this kind can be made.

The babysitter effect

The principle that relative prices govern substitution also gives rise to the *babysitter effect*. Consider a childless couple deciding between a \$20 pizza dinner and a \$200 dinner at a top-end restaurant—a 10:1 price multiple. Later, when they have a child, they will have to hire a babysitter. Suppose this costs \$40. Then the total cost of going to the pizzeria becomes \$60 and to the restaurant \$240—only a 4:1 price multiple. The couple will probably dine out less because of the added childcare expenses.

But whatever dining out they can manage is likely to shift toward higher-end restaurants.

The babysitter effect operates at larger scales, too. Consider a country exporting cars. Shipping costs are almost the same regardless of the quality of the car. So they raise the price of low-end cars relative to that of high-end cars in the destination country. Buyers respond to this; therefore high-end cars constitute a larger proportion of exports than those of the home market.

Time—and other budgets

Price is an important consideration in most people's budgeting decisions. Price may be irrelevant for a lucky few, but everyone faces some kind of other constraints on choice, notably time. The rich may be able to hire others to do chores, but they can't hire anyone else to enjoy a music concert or sport event for them, or to spend quality time with their family. Everyone must choose between competing demands on limited time, just as most people must choose between competing demands on limited income. Indeed, one can think of allocating time using the same ideas of substitution and complementarity as outlined above for allocating money. For example, when washing machines speeded up and simplified home laundry, people cleaned their clothes more often than they had done in the bad old days, but they still spent less total time on laundry work than they used to.

Opportunity cost

The thought process involved in budgeting decisions can be summarized in one general principle. When deciding whether to spend money (or time) on one good or activity, you compare it to other things you could be doing with that money (or time). With a limited income, when you buy a latte at your local coffee shop, you cannot spend that $4 on alternatives like beer or a magazine. This forgone opportunity to do alternative things is the true cost of the latte; that is why in the jargon of economics it is called *opportunity cost*. When making any decision, not just for consumers but also for firms, and often not just in an economic context but also in social, political, and other contexts, the question should be: 'Is this action worth its opportunity cost?'

This relentless insistence on comparing alternatives has made economists the butt of several jokes. Perhaps the oldest of these goes: two economists meet after a long time and are catching up on each other's news. One asks: 'How is your wife?' The other answers: 'Compared to whom?'

This discussion contains another general lesson: almost all of our choices must be made within certain limitations, whether they pertain to money, time, or our networking and information processing ability. Attempting to do one's best within such constraints is the essence of the economics of decision-making.

Risk

Risks pervade our decisions. Allocation of savings among different assets such as equities, bonds, and foreign securities, buying a home, and choices of education, career and spouse, are the biggest risky decisions most of us face. The quality of many goods cannot be perfectly known in advance, so many purchases are also risky. And there are risks of accidents, illness, theft, and so on.

In most contexts, people dislike risk. Not many people would accept a simple bet of winning or losing $100 on the toss of a fair coin. To induce them to accept the bet, either the sum they stand to win must be sufficiently larger than the one they stand to lose, or the odds of winning have to be sufficiently better than 50:50. In other words, their behaviour shows risk-aversion. Risk-aversion is greatly strengthened by *loss-aversion*: most people strongly dislike suffering losses relative to the status quo or some other reference point.

I will mention some other features of decisions under risk later, but I begin with an important consequence of risk-aversion. When faced with a risky prospect, people are willing to pay a premium to insure against it. For example, given a 5 per cent probability of incurring $10,000 in medical bills during the coming year, most people would be willing to pay something more than $500 (statistically, the average loss they would suffer) for insurance that would cover this bill in full.

Suppose Mr A is willing to pay $550. Suppose Ms B takes on Mr A's risk in exchange for a premium of $525. This means Mr A pays Ms B $525 up front. At the end of the year if Mr A has incurred the $10,000 bill, Ms B pays it; otherwise she pays nothing. There is a 95 per cent chance that Ms B simply gets to keep the $525 premium, but a 5 per cent chance that she has to pay the $10,000 thus losing $9,475. As a statistical average, Ms B makes a profit of $0.95 * 525 - 0.05 * 9475 = 498.75 - 473.75 = 25, although of course this is a risky prospect. If Ms B is sufficiently less risk-averse than Mr A, she may like this trade-off between the profit possibility and the risk. Then Mr A and Ms B have the basis for a mutually beneficial trade.

Indeed, this idea of transferring risks to those who are most willing to bear them is probably the most useful role that financial markets play in the economy (although I must admit that in recent years they have played other, less socially useful, roles). We will have occasion to see this in other contexts later.

Ms B might simply dislike risk less than Mr A does, but in practice there are other reasons why Ms B may accept the risk at a lower price than Mr A is willing to pay to avoid it. The most common reason: Ms B actually represents an insurance company *pooling* similar but independent risks for a large number of clients like Mr A. 'Independent' means that there is no common influence on the risks facing different individuals; therefore it is very unlikely that the bills for all or even too many of them will come due at the same time. Very roughly speaking, the 'law of large numbers' says that adding together many independent random outcomes averages out their uncertainty. Using our example, when the company (Ms B's) has many insured clients (like Mr A) with independent risks, close to 5 per cent of the insured clients will incur the large medical bills. Then the company will, with near-certainty, make a profit close to $25 per customer.

The requirement of independence is crucial; common influences that affect all insured risks jointly can defeat pooling with disastrous effects. The great housing bust of 2007–8 in the United States and many other countries exemplifies this. Homeowners may default on their mortgages because of illness or job loss or a family emergency. If default risks are independent across homeowners, they can be insured using pooling. Banks and other mortgage lenders insured their risks using instruments like default swaps. But when the Great Recession struck and house prices fell everywhere, too many homeowners defaulted simultaneously, and mortgage lenders and their insurers faced bankruptcy. Severe recession was the common factor ruining independence, and it had not been adequately recognized or provided for.

The independent risky prospects that can be combined to reduce overall risk don't have to be identical, as with the risks of many similar homeowners above. For example, suppose you have $2 million in savings (very prudent or very lucky you!). You could invest the money in blue-chip stocks, which are due to go up by 60 per cent if the economy as a whole does well, but down by 50 per cent if recession hits. Suppose the two scenarios are equally likely, then you face a 50 per cent risk of losing $1 million. Or you could invest your money in a biotech venture fund, which could double or halve your money with equal chance, so again you have a 50 per cent chance of losing $1 million. Suppose the two risks (a general recession and the success of a specific biotech project) are independent, then you can reduce your overall risk by *diversification* of your portfolio: holding a mix of the two. Suppose you invest $1 million in each. Now you will lose 50 per cent only if both outcomes are bad, which happens with only a 25 per cent chance, like two fair coins independently tossed both coming tails up. Table 2 shows the results of the three investment strategies in each of the four possible scenarios. Observe how the downside—your wealth falling to $1 million—has been reduced from two scenarios to one, reducing its probability from 50 per cent to 25 per cent. Of course the upside is now smaller: you will never reach $4 million. But if you are risk-averse (and perhaps also loss-averse), as you should be with all your retirement savings at stake, you will probably accept the trade-off. Note that blue-chip stocks have a role in your portfolio because they provide diversification, even though on their own they look worse than does the biotech fund: the two have the same downside risk (50 per cent loss), while blue chips have a smaller upside gain than biotech (60 per cent against 100 per cent).

Finally, one risk can be reduced by taking another risk that is negatively correlated with the first, in other words, one that has a bad outcome when the first has a good outcome and vice versa. The good and bad of the two partly offset each other, leaving you with less risk overall. This is called *hedging*. As a trivial example, at the next Super Bowl or World Cup Final, you can bet against the team you favour, so if it loses you at least have the consolation

Table 2. Reducing risk of loss by diversification

Portfolio	Both up	Blue chip up, biotech down	Biotech up, blue chip down	Both down
Blue chip	3.2	3.2	1.0	1.0
Biotech	4.0	1.0	4.0	1.0
Mix	3.6	2.1	2.5	1.0

of money won from your bet. More seriously, if your job and income depend on the success of one sector of the economy, your portfolio should have assets that do well when this sector does poorly. Investing your pension fund in the stock of the company where you work exposes you to great risk—loss of both income and wealth—if the company does badly. For diversification you should do the opposite: sell short some of its stock, in other words, commit to selling the stock at an agreed future date at an agreed price, so you will profit if the stock falls below this agreed price. Similar effects can be achieved using options, which give you the right but not the obligation to sell. Of course, owning your company's shares may have offsetting good effect on incentives, which can be important for top management, but less so for ordinary workers or even middle managers in the firm, each of whom can do little to affect the share price. I discuss this further in Chapter 3 in the section 'Firms as organizations'.

Are consumers rational?

Conventional economic theory assumed that consumers (and indeed all participants in the economy, including managers of firms, etc.) make their decisions rationally. This means that they know their own preferences, and given the choice among any alternatives, they calculate which one they like best and choose it. Psychologists and other social scientists always found this difficult to believe. For a long time the standard economic counterargument was that the rational choice approach works: it gives good explanations of market behaviour of aggregates of consumers over reasonable time-spans, and can be thought of as *as if* the consumers were acting rationally. But evidence of departure from conventional rationality (actual or as if) has mounted from widely different sources including laboratory experiments, field observations, and imaging of brain activity in the decision-making process, and this is found to affect outcomes of transactions and markets in many contexts. Therefore mainstream economics has accepted and internalized many of the criticisms. The new view, often called 'behavioural economics', has supplemented conventional theories and in some cases modified and replaced them.

Definitive consensus has yet to emerge, but the most broadly accepted framework is one developed and advocated by psychologist Daniel Kahneman, who shared the 2002 economics Nobel prize for his work. He recognizes two systems the brain uses for making decisions. He calls these System I and System II to avoid prejudicial connotations. System I is fast, instinctive, and uses heuristics (trial-and-error-based automatic decision rules) instead of explicit calculation for each situation. System II is slower and makes explicit calculations, closer to the picture in conventional economics. System I has obvious merits. It saves calculation cost and time in routine decisions–and also in emergencies such as fleeing from predators. Therefore it may have emerged in the process of human evolution by natural selection. It may also play a role in impulsive decisions. The systems do not exist in separate watertight compartments: the heuristics of System I are modified over time as a result of experience and calculation, and use of System II in repeated situations generates new heuristics that are then incorporated into System I.

Even when someone wants to think about a decision in the consciously calculating framework of System II, the required information and the complexity of the calculation may prevent him or her from doing a perfect job of it. This may be especially important in decisions of the poor, who have too many things to think about: juggling multiple jobs, how the cost of every single item can fit into their limited budgets, and so on.

Perhaps the most important finding of Kahneman and others is that consumers care not only about what they finally ended up with, but also how it compares to some *reference point*, which depending on the context can be their status quo level of income or consumption, the level they regard as normal in their community, or some other standard of comparison. People regard falling below the reference point by say $100 as far more serious than an equal gain above it; this is the phenomenon of *loss-aversion*. This may occur because the loss hits System I emotions harder, but it could also figure in System II calculations because the status quo or comparisons with peers do genuinely affect preferences.

The status quo also plays a role in the *endowment effect*, where people place an extra value on something they own by the mere fact of ownership. Laboratory experiments have shown that people's willingness to pay for a small object like a coffee mug (where the status quo is no ownership) is significantly less than their willingness to accept money to give it up after owning it for as little as 20 minutes. This is probably a System I feature; habitual traders who have less attachment to objects they trade are found to be less prone to the endowment effect.

Reference points can be created and manipulated by *framing* choices in different ways. The most dramatic example is where people regard two disasters, one in which 400 lives are lost and the other in which 600 lives are at risk but 200 are saved, as different. This is probably another System I feature; slower logical thought would make them recognize that the difference is not substantive.

Many people turn down economic gain because of perceived unfairness or because the situation provokes emotions like anger. This could be cold calculation in System II, but functional magnetic resonance imaging (fMRI) studies of people making such decisions show activity in parts of the brain normally associated with System I and deep emotions. The prime example is the 'ultimatum game'. Of two players A and B, one, say A, is chosen at random to propose division of a sum like $10 between the two. If B accepts A's proposal, it is implemented; if B rejects it, neither gets anything. Cold economic logic suggests that B's choice is between something and nothing, and so B should therefore accept whatever A offers, even if it is just one penny. In fact many Bs reject anything short of about $3. And anticipating this, or driven by their own sense of fairness, most As offer more, quite often an equal split. If the role of proposer is not randomly assigned, but based on scores in a prior puzzle-solving contest, many B's are willing to accept smaller shares—presumably because they think A's success in the contest has earned him or her the right to a higher share!

In decisions involving time, people often exhibit inconsistency. They show high impatience in decisions over the immediate future, while claiming to be more patient in matters farther off. They will consume right now, planning to save or diet next year. Of course, when next year comes, immediate impatience kicks in again. In this they are just following the example of St Augustine, who asked of god: 'Give me chastity and continence, but not yet'.

Finally, people are not purely selfish; their behaviour shows empathy and concern for fairness and equity. They make choices that benefit others—certainly for family and close friends, but also for strangers—at some cost to themselves. This behaviour may have been hardwired in an evolutionary process for group survival, or deliberately instilled by socialization and education, or some combination of the two. People's preferences are heavily influenced by the society and culture in which they live and were brought up, by what their immediate friends think, and so on.

Given the space constraint, I must limit myself to listing these few departures from the economist's picture of perfect individual rationality, and turn to discuss some consequences. The new findings do not generally contradict very broad features of aggregate behaviour in markets for most everyday commodities. Instinctive behaviour usually does not contradict the 'law of demand' that when a price of something rises, less of it is demanded, but the magnitude and time-lag of the response can be affected. And loss-aversion and other features of decisions under risk can affect the properties of financial markets in significant ways.

When analysing transactions involving two or more individuals, behavioural aspects become more important. Participants in such transactions must think how their partners or opponents would actually behave, and not assume conventionally rational responses, if they are to do well in the game of strategy that is played out in such contexts. Some problems of market design, for example auctions, also involve game-theoretic considerations, and good understanding of participants' behaviour becomes essential for good design.

Policy-makers can use research on framing, immediate impatience, and limited will-power to 'nudge' the population into actions that would be in their own System II interest, such as healthy lifestyles and prudent saving. For example, many people find it mentally costly to evaluate multiple plans for saving, or are affected by immediate impatience, and end up choosing none. Making some basic plan the status quo or default option (instead of no plan) can overcome the calculation cost problem, and getting people to commit now to a saving plan that starts at a later date can counter their immediate impatience. Experiments have shown that such policies are more effective than educating people about the importance of saving or subsidizing saving. Framing and nudging can also be effective in getting people to make 'green' choices that are better for the environment. If green choices are the default option, some consumers will stay with it. Loss-aversion, where a loss in relation to the reference point looms bigger than an equal gain, also comes into play. Green choices are often somewhat more costly than non-green ones. If the default option is non-green, then making a green choice would mean accepting a loss; consumers are likely to avoid this. If the default option is green, switching to a non-green choice would bring an equal gain, but consumers are less likely to go for it.

Thus behavioural economics helps policy-makers design default options cleverly to alter consumer behaviour. This is paternalism, but of a mild or soft kind: it can help consumers overcome their short-term or System I temptations, and thereby achieve outcomes that may be in their own best calculated long-run or System II interests. However, we must recognize the potential for abuse—the state may use the same methods to encroach dangerously on individual freedom. Here as in all public policy matters, citizens must exercise eternal vigilance on policy-makers.

Chapter 3
Producers

Costs

At its most general, production is an activity that transforms inputs—raw materials and other produced goods, as well as services of labour, land, and capital—into outputs. Anyone organizing this activity must pay attention to the costs of these inputs—the prices of inputs that are used up, as well as wages, rents, and costs of capital (interest and depreciation). A producer seeking profits wants to keep costs low; non-profit and public-sector producers also want to be cost-effective and have limited budgets. Decisions of whether to produce, how much to produce, and the appropriate mix of inputs to be used, all depend on costs.

Most production decisions have multiple stages. At the earliest stage, costs must be incurred to set up the organization, usually a firm, which will carry out the production activity. In most advanced countries this cost is trivial, but as a World Bank report (<http://www.doingbusiness.org/rankings>) shows, in many less-developed countries it can be very substantial, in both money and time. Next comes the cost of acquiring land, office space, machinery, etc. The amount varies greatly depending on the nature of the activity. A petrochemical plant needs huge capital investment; a small garment-making shop can rent a room and a few sewing machines. Next, in some businesses, large expenditures are needed before anything can be produced at all. For example, software for operating systems, browsers, application programs, and games must be developed and tested before a single copy can be sold; hence the name first-copy costs. Finally, actual production involves costs of labour, materials, and so on, followed by those of marketing; these are a large part of the costs of garments, but a small part for computer software.

Decisions at each stage—whether to enter this business, the scale at which to enter, and so on—must look ahead to the prospects of recovering the costs, or making a profit. At each stage, some of the costs must be committed or *sunk*, in the sense that they cannot be recouped if something goes wrong and the subsequent stages have to be aborted. Therefore the decisions at the remaining stages should consider only whether the costs not yet sunk can be recovered.

For example, a retail garment store must rent its premises, keep some stock on hand, and hire some staff. If it fails to make any sales, it cannot recoup these costs (unless it has some return privileges for the stock). Therefore at this point all these costs are sunk, and the extra cost of the actual act of selling a dress, say, is almost zero. Should the owner therefore be willing to sell the dress to you if you offer $1 for it? No; other customers willing to pay more might show up tomorrow. Every action must be compared with all possible alternatives, and taken only if it is better than all the rest. Therefore the true cost of selling the dress today is an opportunity cost: the cost of giving up the opportunity to sell it tomorrow or later. That is uncertain; therefore if you try to bargain with the owner for a better price, the owner's decision involves some intricate estimation and calculation of these opportunities and risks. That is one reason why stores have non-negotiable fixed prices and rarely give lower-level employees any power to bargain with customers. The garment store may discount its merchandise drastically at the end of the season, as do sellers of perishable fruit or vegetables in farmers' markets at the end of the day, because the opportunity cost of forgoing future sales is very low at that point.

This brief general discussion suffices to show that cost calculations are not simply matters of arithmetic to be totted up in a ledger or a spreadsheet; they involve much judgement about uncertain prospects.

How costs enter into firms' decisions depends on the nature of the market. Let us consider various possibilities.

Small firms: supply curves

Producers in some markets are so small that individually they cannot influence the price, which is determined by larger forces of supply and demand in the whole market. Farmers in most agricultural markets, and most mining and petroleum producing firms, are in this situation. Each such firm has only one basic decision to make: how much to produce at the going price.

For profit-seeking firms, one general principle governs this decision: expand the operation so long as the addition to revenue from the added quantity exceeds the extra cost of supplying it (the technical term in the jargon of economics is *marginal cost*). But correct interpretation of marginal cost depends on the context, in other words, on the precise 'margin' at which the decision is being made. At a final stage when all costs have been sunk, the marginal cost may be zero or very small; as a train or airplane is ready to depart with some empty seats, the marginal cost of another passenger is virtually zero. But at an earlier stage, when the decision is whether to schedule that train or the flight, the marginal cost includes all the crew and fuel costs and any opportunity cost of using the equipment for this purpose rather than on some other route. Finally, at the earliest stage when considering whether to set up or expand the rail company or the airline, the marginal cost includes the opportunity cost of using capital for this purpose rather than another, say a pharmaceutical firm.

In many cases, the marginal cost rises with the quantity. For example, a mining operation starts with the most easily accessible or richest deposits, and only then moves on to the ones that are more difficult and therefore more costly to extract; a farmer cultivates the best land first, and expands output by gradually turning to less productive land. This process naturally brings expansion to an end at any given price. Eventually the marginal cost catches up with the price, making further expansion unprofitable. That determines the firm's choice of quantity (its supply) at that price. We can then show the relationship between price and the total quantity supplied in the market, in other words a (market) supply curve, just as we graphed a market demand curve coming from buyers' decisions.

In other cases marginal cost decreases (or at least does not increase) as quantity increases, so further expansion becomes even more profitable at a given price. For example, once the first-copy costs of software development are sunk, the marginal cost of printing and mailing a CD are minimal, and the marginal cost of a web-based download is almost zero; the cost of building a petrochemical plant increases less than proportionately with its capacity, so the marginal cost of successively larger capacity decreases. In such cases one or a few firms grow to the point where they constitute a large fraction of the market, and each has some influence over the price. Then the strategic analysis of the next section becomes relevant. For now, let us stay with the case where each firm's quantity at a given price is such a small part of the market that it has no power to influence the price.

The construction of the market supply curve is simply a mirror image of that of the market demand curve we saw in the previous

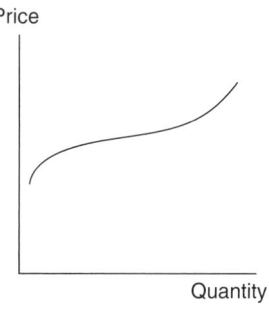

Price

Quantity

5. A market supply curve

chapter. Figure 5 gives an example. The curve slopes upward, because at higher prices more firms find it profitable to enter this market, to expand their plants, run more shifts, or engage in more selling efforts, depending on the time span involved and on the specifics of production and selling in their industry. At a very low price, just a few firms with superior proprietary technology, land, or other resources may be able to supply, so the lower left portion of the curve has low price-responsiveness. At somewhat higher prices, many firms with standard general technologies enter the picture, so the price responsiveness is higher and the curve is flatter. Finally, at the right hand end, the industry hits capacity limitations and price-responsiveness decreases again.

Just as a market demand curve shifts because of changes in some background variables such as consumer incomes or prices of substitutes or complements, a supply curve can shift because of changes in costs of inputs or technical progress. Figure 6 gives an example of the latter. The shift is bigger on the right hand side of the curve than on the left: the idea is that the left end of the curve corresponds to firms that are already at the technological frontier and do not benefit much from further advances, while other firms benefit by catching up as well as from new advances, so their costs decrease more.

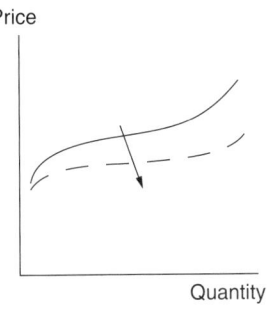

Price

Quantity

6. Shift of the supply curve

We can also develop some general ideas about when supply curves will be flatter, in other words more price-responsive (elastic) as in the left panel of Figure 7, or steeper, in other words less price responsive (inelastic) as in the right hand panel. Some examples of high price-responsiveness are: (i) If the time span is long, more firms can enter or exit, and existing firms can make more adjustments in their production plans. (ii) In industries with standard technologies to which all firms have easy access, a small price increase around their common level of unit cost will generate a large quantity response. (iii) If a price increase in extractive industries is believed to be temporary, firms expect to profit by producing more right now and will respond rapidly to the increase. Low price responsiveness arises in the opposite circumstances, and in some other situations. For example, if the whole industry hits a capacity constraint (limit to available land or a transport bottleneck) then the price incentive cannot bring forth greater supply.

These examples are not meant to be definitive or exhaustive; they are merely intended to spur your thinking about situations you may have experienced or observed. In Chapter 4, I will put together the ideas about demand and supply curves to help you understand the operation of markets.

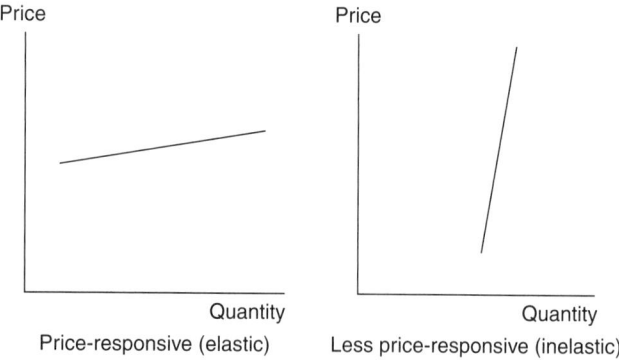

Price-responsive (elastic) · Less price-responsive (inelastic)

7. **More and less price-responsive market supply curves**

In Chapter 2, the concepts were illustrated using a statistical estimation of aggregate consumer demand. A similar economy-wide supply curve would be less meaningful in microeconomics. Industry-specific, statistically estimated cost curves do exist, but even they fail to bring out the role of individual firms. Therefore I will illustrate cost and supply curves using an example based on reality but without supporting statistical evidence.

Consider the short-term supply curve for crude oil. At this stage, new exploration and development of reserves is not a consideration, and those costs are sunk. The marginal costs of production are those of maintenance and operation of the existing wells and related equipment and facilities to bring the oil to the surface (these are called *lifting costs* in the jargon of the industry), and supply is limited by the capacity of the existing wells. Cost and capacity data are available for some countries; these are shown in Table 3.

Figure 8 shows the same information graphically in a supply curve, where each country or region is willing to produce a quantity up to its capacity when the price exceeds its marginal cost.

Table 3. Crude oil lifting costs and capacities, 2009

Country or Region	Lifting costs per barrel	Capacity (million barrels/day)	Total capacity upto this cost
Central and South America	6.21	10.28	10.28
Middle East	9.89	24.27	34.55
Africa	10.31	9.36	43.91
United States	12.18	8.62	52.53
Canada	12.69	3.40	55.93

Source: Cost data from <http://www.eia.gov/tools/faqs/faq.cfm?id=367&t=6>, capacity data from <http://www.eia.gov/forecasts/steo/data.cfm?type=tables>, Tables 3b and 3c

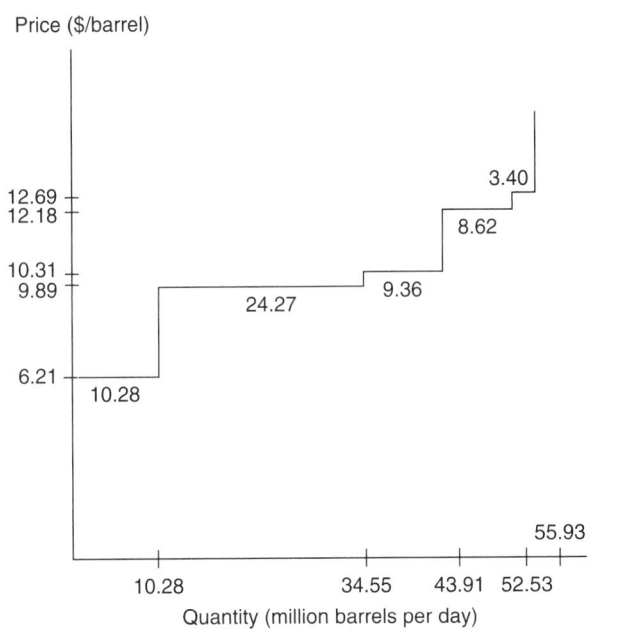

8. **An illustrative short-run supply curve for crude oil**

Although this example makes the idea of a supply curve stand out vividly, it is merely illustrative. First, data are not available for all countries; for example Russia and China are omitted for want of cost data. Second, countries or regions are not the right unit of analysis. Ideally we should have data on lifting costs and capacities for all the thousands of individual wells. These differ greatly within a country; they would generate a smooth supply curve instead of the large steps shown. Finally and most importantly, lifting costs are not correct short-run marginal costs. Firms that operate the wells have the choice of leaving oil in the ground, thus producing at less than full capacity, if they believe that prices will rise in the future. In other words, opportunity costs are the correct measure. But these are based on expectations and calculations done within firms, and are not available in reported data. Therefore this example can be used to improve understanding of the ideas, but should not be taken literally.

The decision of how much to produce or supply is subtle and complex in many ways. Except for custom production to order, the decision must be made without knowing the exact demand. If you produce too much, you run the risk of failing to sell all; if too little, you run the risk of disappointing and alienating some customers. Firms would not be willing to produce more unless they could expect to recoup the costs. In affluent market economies consumers are willing to pay a higher price to get assured availability, and competitive firms profit from catering to them. That helps explain why my local coffee shop almost never runs out of goodies. In socialist economies, producers suffer no penalty for disappointing customers; on the contrary they enjoy some power by being able to allocate scarce goods to favoured customers. That helps explain why those economies always suffer shortages.

Pricing strategies

When a firm can influence the price in its market, it must devise pricing strategies for its interaction with customers as well as with competing firms. I will focus on private-sector firms whose main objective is profit; related but different analyses apply to non-profit or public enterprises.

The customers of any firm differ in the satisfaction they get from its products relative to other things on which they could spend their money, and therefore differ in their willingness to pay for its products. A profit-seeking firm would benefit by serving any customer who pays more than the marginal cost of the service. But it does not want to give the same deal to other customers who are willing to pay more. Firms' attempts to extract from each customer the full amount that he or she is willing to pay explain many pricing strategies we observe.

Airlines provide the best-known example. Business travellers are willing to pay higher prices than are tourists or people visiting family. Airlines would like to attract the latter types with low fares without offering the same deals to business types, but cannot do so directly. Blatant discrimination probably would be illegal and is certainly impractical. Any obvious indicators—having your company's travel office make the reservation, wearing a suit, and so on—can easily be circumvented. So airlines exploit other differences between the types: business travellers want flexibility, while tourists and family travellers are willing to make advance purchases and commit themselves to a schedule; business travellers (actually, their companies) are more willing to pay for the comfort of business- or first-class on long hauls; and so on. Therefore airlines offer different types of tickets: cheap, advance purchase, non-refundable economy (cattle-class) tickets, and high-priced, business- or first-class, unrestricted tickets. When the prices are calculated and set in just the right way, each type of traveller selects the type of ticket and service the airline intends for him or her.

This strategy of separating or 'screening' different buyers with different willingness to pay by offering different versions of the product at different prices and letting them select one is called *screening by self-selection*. Once you understand this method of price-discrimination you will see it everywhere. The following are just a few examples.

Computer software often comes in a professional or business version and a lite or student version. The latter is lower priced but has fewer features. Companies usually buy the first kind: they believe their employees need all the features, or that they should have them just in case they need them later. Price is less of a concern for them. Casual users paying out of their own pockets are more likely to be satisfied with only the basic features. Vendors can profit by separating the two types and charging each a price closer to the buyers' willingness to pay. How is the lite version made? Usually by taking the full version and disabling the advanced features! So the price difference has nothing to do with any additional cost of programming the advanced features; its sole purpose is to achieve more profitable screening.

Coffee shops serve two types of customers, regulars and transients. Regulars are more likely to respond to price differences among different coffee shops in town, because over the year their savings will amount to quite a lot. Transients are likely to go to the first one they find on the street and not spend time searching for a lower price. To separate the two, the shop sets a high price and gives 'buy 10, get one free' loyalty cards. More generally, quantity discounts can serve a similar purpose.

Insurance companies would like to charge higher premiums per dollar of coverage to the applicants whose risks are higher. Some risks can be assessed and premiums charged accordingly: smokers, homeowners in flood-prone areas, and so on, pay more for insurance. Other risks require screening by self-selection. People often have a better idea of their own risk than does the insurance company, and those with higher risk are less willing to bear the risk themselves. Therefore versions of insurance policies can help separate them. Policies with high deductible or co-insurance but low premiums are more appealing to the low-risk types who don't expect to have to use the service often. The high-risk types are keener to avoid having to pay more or they are more often out of pocket, so they prefer policies with fuller coverage even though the premiums are higher. With suitably designed premiums and co-pays in separate packages, insurance companies can separate the two types and enjoy higher profits.

Issuers of credit cards have three types of potential customers. From their perspective, those likely to default are the worst, but those who pay off the whole account every month are almost equally bad. Those who run revolving balances and pay a lot of interest are the best. The issuers developed a clever strategy to attract selectively these profitable types: an offer to transfer balances from another card at an attractively low interest rate for the first few months. Obviously this appeals to those who have run up balances and are paying higher interest charges elsewhere.

Such strategies have limitations. They do not extract from each and every buyer his or her full willingness to pay, usually for the simple reason that sellers do not have this information. The strategies must be coarser, like the airline's two-fare strategy above. Within each type there is heterogeneity of willingness to pay. For example business fliers' (or their firms') willingness to pay for flexibility and comfort will vary between top- and middle-level managers, and from one company to another. The two-fare strategy does not exploit such fine detail, but it works well enough for airlines to increase their profits (or reduce their losses). Vendors on the internet now have so much information about individual buyers from their previous purchases and other databases that they can attempt perfect price discrimination: when you log into their site, they instantly estimate your willingness to pay and display an individually tailored price to extract it all. Car insurance companies can use data from 'telematic' devices (see <http://en.wikipedia.org/wiki/Telematics>) in the car to monitor the driver's actions in great detail, and find premiums precisely tailored to his or her skill and care.

There are further limitations. First, discrimination is not possible if buyers can easily resell the good or service—so anyone can pretend to be a low-paying customer and then resell to others undercutting the price the firm wants to charge them. Next, discrimination based on some observable differences among consumers, such as age or gender, may be illegal or socially unacceptable. Third, screening by self-selection cannot go so far that buyers with higher willingness to pay settle for the cheaper version. For example the difference between business and economy fares cannot exceed the extra value business fliers place on the extra comfort; therefore the firm may be unable to extract their full willingness to pay. But some profitable discrimination is feasible, and is frequently used.

Some pricing strategies exploit insights from behavioural economics. Recall Kahneman's finding that people often make decisions using the instinctive System I. In purchase decisions they focus on the most visible major item of information about a product without taking the time and effort to investigate other seemingly minor matters. Therefore sellers highlight a bargain price, hiding other charges that customers discover only when it is too late. Airlines publicize low fares, concealing baggage fees, payments for inflight food and drink, and so on. One airline even planned to charge passengers for using lavatories on its aircraft, but retreated when that attracted too much bad publicity. Many hotels advertise attractively low room rates. Only when guests are settled in do they discover how much more they must pay for internet access, use of the fitness room, and so on.

Firms' responses to inflation exploit the behavioural trait that prices are more visible than some other attributes of products.

A price rise, even if justified by cost increases, might deter some consumers. Instead, where possible firms keep the price and outer appearance of the package unchanged, but quietly and gradually reduce the contents: fewer or smaller cookies, for example. When this has gone too far to pass unnoticed, they raise the price in a jump, using as their justification an increase in contents (actually only back to the original level!).

Rivalry among large firms

Unless a firm is so small in its market that its sole decision is how much to produce at the going price, it must be aware of its rival firms and strategize against, or sometimes jointly with, them. The first step in such strategic thinking is the recognition that rival firms are strategizing similarly and simultaneously.

First, let us look at a little of the terminology you will meet, not only in economics books but also in business newspapers and magazines. A market with only one firm is called a *monopoly*, from the Greek *monos* (single, alone); *poleein* (to sell). (Its mirror-image, a single firm on the buying side of a market, is a monopsony.) Governments grant monopoly rights for limited periods to inventors through patents, and to authors and creators of software through copyrights, but also to favoured firms or in exchange for political contributions or bribes. A market with a small number of firms (usually fewer than ten) is called an *oligopoly* (Greek *oligos* (little, few)). If oligopolists collude to keep prices high and new competitors out of their market they are said to form a *cartel*. Such practices, at least if carried out explicitly, are illegal in most countries, and antitrust policies try to keep markets competitive. It is not easy to define what constitutes 'a market' because most things have some substitutes and ultimately everything competes for the consumer's budget, but approximate and porous boundaries can be drawn for purposes of economic analysis and antitrust policy.

Strategic interaction in oligopoly can be understood using game theory. The game of competition among such firms is usually a *prisoners' dilemma*. In the story that gives the game its name, the police have arrested two people whom they could convict of a minor crime, but suspect them to be guilty of a much more serious crime. They interrogate the two separately, and invite each to confess also implicating the other. Each will get leniency if he or she confesses while the other holds out, but an especially harsh sentence if matters are the other way round. Therefore each finds it in his or her own interest to confess, regardless of what he or she thinks the other will do. But when both confess they are both convicted of the bigger crime, which is worse for both than the sentence for the minor crime that they would get if neither confessed.

In an oligopoly, each firm is tempted to compete to win customers at the expense of other firms by offering a lower price, a better product, more after-sales service, advertising, and so on. If the other firms do not use such competitive strategies, the one that does gets a big advantage; if others do, the one that does not is left behind. But when all compete, their actions defeat each other. They become prisoners of a dilemma: all end up with lower prices or higher costs, and lower profits. Of course the consumers benefit from price competition, and as we shall see in Chapter 4, competition promotes overall social efficiency. But the firms do lose. To resolve their dilemma, they must devise ways to promise credibly to one another not to compete so hard. Conversely, if antitrust policy has the overall social interest as its objective, it should anticipate and prevent attempts by firms to collude.

Firms compete with others that are already *in* the relevant market; they compete as hard or harder *for* the market. When a dominant position in a lucrative market is at stake, for example when airwave spectrum for mobile phones in a big city is being sold, competing firms bid aggressively for that right, dissipating the profits they stand to make. Some such dilemmas may also hurt overall social benefit. If one firm beats another by one day in a race to invent and patent a mass-market drug to treat a condition like high cholesterol or erectile dysfunction, the benefit to society is small—because the treatment is simply available for one extra day—but the benefit to the patent-winning firm is huge: 20 years of monopoly profit. Therefore such R&D competition is often carried to excess. Competition for lucrative illegal markets, such as territories for drug-dealing or gambling, can be literally cut-throat.

Can firms avoid these prisoners' dilemmas? A primary requirement is an ongoing and stable interaction. Suppose the firms in an industry have reached an agreement to keep prices high. Such agreements are mostly unenforceable at law; in fact explicit collusion is illegal under most countries' antitrust laws. Therefore any implicit agreement has to be self-sustaining. Each firm is tempted to undercut the agreed price and increase its own profit at the expense of other firms. But it risks tit-for-tat retaliatory price cuts by the others, leading to a collapse of the arrangement and then lower profits for all including itself. It must weigh the immediate profit gain against the risk of future loss. If it expects a stable and ongoing interaction, the long run will be more important in its calculation, and it is likely to desist from breaking the agreement. But if the industry is declining or likely to be rendered obsolete by technical change, or if the agreement is likely to be upset by newcomers who are not part of it, then the firm may go for the short-run advantage by cutting its price. Of course when all firms do this, the dilemma strikes.

Firms do try explicit collusion in violation of antitrust laws; probably the best-known recent example, vividly described in *The Informant* by Kurt Eichenwald, was the market for lysine, a chemical widely used in animal-feed. Executives of the leading firms, Archer Daniels Midland of the US and Ajinomoto of Japan, met to negotiate, keep prices high, and divide up the market. Of course the customers suffered. The conspirators' private slogan was: 'The competitors are our friends, and the customers are our enemies'.

Firms also think up some ingenious devices for implicit collusion. For example, in a round of US mobile telephone spectrum auctions in multiple area codes, bidders communicated their special interest in particular areas by adding the last three digits of that area code to bids; for example $10,000,415 says to other bidders that I am willing to fight hard for area code 415 (San Francisco), so you had better stay out. Other firms might have special stakes in other areas. The messages enable them to divide up the whole market and avoid competition in each area.

Entrenched monopolists or oligopolists wish to deter new entrants, who would dilute their market power. They can threaten to start a price war that would make entry unprofitable. But mere words may be seen as empty threats; they have to be made credible. One device is to set a price lower than the existing market power would justify, the aim being to convince a prospective entrant that the incumbent firms' costs are very low, so the entrant would find the competition too fierce. The incumbent firms can also maintain a large capacity, so they can easily expand output and start a price war should a new entrant appear. This strategy manipulates costs: by making the commitment to high capacity, in other words sinking the capacity cost, the firm lowers the marginal cost of future expansion.

The record of success in creating and sustaining cartels over a long haul has not been very good. The crude petroleum cartel OPEC achieved notoriety in the 1970s. But cheating by some of its smaller members, increased production from nonmembers, and buyers' actions to decrease their oil-dependence reduced OPEC's market power within a decade. Attempts of other commodity and mining industries to mimic OPEC were nonstarters or very short-lived. China recently tried to exert monopoly over rare-earth elements, which are vital for cutting-edge technologies including computers, smartphones, and weaponry. But supplies from other countries are quickly emerging, technological improvements are reducing the amounts of the elements needed in these devices, and recycling is reducing the need for new supplies, thereby eroding China's market power. The diamond cartel organized by the firm of De Beers is probably the only one to have survived and flourished for almost a century. That required eternal vigilance to absorb some new producers and deter others, create and sustain a market by imaginative advertising, and to avoid competition from sales of pre-owned diamonds by inducing a mindset in diamond owners never to resell, or making it possible to sell only at a great loss.

Supply chains

Buyers are not always final consumers. Production of most goods involves several stages and assembly of different components. The output of one stage is sold to another firm that will process it and combine it with other inputs; firms buy components made by other firms. As containerization and air-freight lowered transport costs and international trade regimes became more liberal, supply chains went global in the 1990s and early 2000s, although recent years have seen some retreat from extreme outsourcing. Transactions where both buyers and sellers are firms constitute at least as important a part of the overall market economy as do sales to final consumers. Management of supply chains is almost as important a part of firms' activities as organization of their own production.

If the items one firm sells to another are standardized commodities, for example fuel or RAM memory chips, then the transactions fall within the scope of standard supply and demand analysis. The demand curve in this case comes from firms, not consumers, but the principle of substitution applies and the law of demand holds. But more often the items are not standardized; the buying firm has specific requirements, for example a machine to serve a particular purpose or custom software, and the items must be designed to meet them. The transaction requires a contract between the two firms, and its terms are subject to bilateral negotiation. The price can be affected by their relative bargaining powers, which in turn depend on their alternative opportunities: the buying firm may have other potential sources and the selling firm other potential contracts it could enter into. Once the contract is made, the two firms are to some extent stuck with each other. No contract can anticipate and cover all possible contingencies. Therefore each firm has some wiggle room, which it can opportunistically exploit to its own advantage and at the expense of the partner. All this makes the operation and the analysis of inter-firm transactions much more complex than simple supply and demand. In this brief introduction I cannot develop details, but one important implication follows.

Firms as organizations

Firms buy some inputs to their production from other firms and make some inputs in-house. The choice is theirs, and thinking about it raises some intriguing and basic questions.

As I mentioned in Chapter 1 and will discuss in more detail in Chapter 4, the market provides good information and incentives through the price system. Then why not leave everything to the market? Why not produce each tiny link of the supply chain in a separate firm, which sells its output in a market to another firm that makes the next link? Or why not do exactly the opposite: make everything in-house? Carrying this thought to its logical limit, why not have just one firm, Gross Domestic Products Inc., for the nation's economy?

Ronald Coase suggested the answer, and Oliver Williamson enriched and developed it; both won Nobel prizes for their contributions. The key idea is that using markets entails significant costs. Most goods transacted between firms have to be tailored to the specific needs of the buyer. Therefore the buyer must locate a suitable supplier, and negotiate a contract. The contract cannot specify every contingency in detail. Then each party can engage in opportunistic behaviour, for example cutting costs and shading quality a little, or demanding alteration of the terms of the contract in its favour when the other party can no longer find a new partner. Therefore contractual performance must be monitored, disputes negotiated or ultimately settled in court, and so on. All these things are costly. In some countries the court may be slow, inefficient, biased, or corrupt; then contracts must be self-enforcing based on long-term reputations and relationships, which require costly build-up and maintenance. All such costs, called *transaction costs*, can be just as important as ordinary costs of production.

In-house production also involves transaction costs, but of a different kind. The information and incentives that would be contained in the market price have to be replicated internally. The firm as a whole profits by responding to a higher price: expanding production and doing so in a cost-efficient way. To transfer this incentive to individual managers, their compensation has to include some profit-sharing. That is a cost to the firm's ultimate owners, the shareholders. Workers' performance may have to be monitored. Such internal transaction costs of corporate governance rise rapidly with the size and depth of the managerial hierarchy. Incentivizing the managers, monitoring the workers, monitoring the monitors, preventing collusion among the lower tiers of workers and managers to defeat upper tiers' strategies to make them work harder and smarter—all these get harder and costlier, limiting the firm's span of control. Running the whole economy as one firm becomes virtually impossible and hugely counterproductive; failure of central planning in communist countries gives conclusive proof of this.

A firm's make-or-buy decision has to consider transaction costs of the two modes in addition to the ordinary costs of internal production and the price of buying from another firm, and choose the mode that has lower overall cost. The result will vary depending on the context. Therefore we see some highly integrated firms that make almost everything in-house, some who merely design their products and do some final assembly, outsourcing almost all manufacturing, and many somewhere between these extremes. Many petroleum companies exemplify integration. An oil field and a refinery connected by a pipeline are stuck with each other; it would be very costly for one to switch to a relationship with another firm. Therefore risks of opportunistic behaviour are large; they are most easily mitigated by bringing both operations within one company. Some makers of desktop computers and many garment and shoe companies exemplify the opposite extreme: 'hollow' companies that do almost no manufacturing. Their components are standardized, the quality of their suppliers can be monitored relatively easily, and they can relatively easily switch to other suppliers even in other countries if necessary. Therefore transaction costs are low, and they can outsource manufacturing to the lowest-wage sources.

Firms don't always get the make-or-buy decision right; many have sent manufacturing offshore to low-wage countries only to find that the advantage of low labour costs was wiped out by quality problems, costs and delays in transporting the product to markets back home, greater risks of supply disruption, risks in contract enforcement, and loss of synergies of proximity between R&D, design, production, and business processing. Labour cost advantage of countries like China is also eroding as their wages rise faster than those in the US.

The transaction cost perspective also helps explain the large conglomerates we find in many less-developed countries. These are often family-owned, and span things with little in common: textiles, chemicals, cars, beverages, hotels, information technology services, and more. A rationale can be found in the defective legal system of these countries. Formal contract enforcement is unreliable; business dealings are governed by reputation and relationships. If your company has accumulated profits but the best new investments are in some other line of business, you cannot lend out the capital to an unconnected firm and hope for honest return on your investment. Instead you bring that activity under the umbrella of your own family firm, where relational aspects are strongest. The conglomerate need not create any synergies or conventional efficiencies in production. Instead it reduces governance costs.

Chapter 4
Markets

Supply and demand

Thomas Carlyle supposedly said: 'Teach a parrot the terms supply and demand and you've got an economist.' As with many such glib sayings, this gets at only the starting point of an intricate and even beautiful mechanism, but it is a good place to start. Although economics has become much more mathematical, the simple diagrammatic apparatus of supply and demand curves, which goes back a century and owes much to the writings of the British economist Alfred Marshall, remains the basic tool in most economists' thinking.

In Chapters 2 and 3, we met demand and supply curves. Now put together the demand and supply curves for some commodity, say coffee, into one diagram, as shown in Figure 9. The two curves meet at the point labelled E, which corresponds to price P and quantity Q. If price P prevails in the market, the quantity demanded by consumers equals the quantity supplied by the producers, namely Q. Supply equals demand; the market clears; we have equilibrium.

What process or mechanism might bring about this price? The simple answer goes as follows. If the price is higher than P, then at that price the quantity that producers are willing to supply will

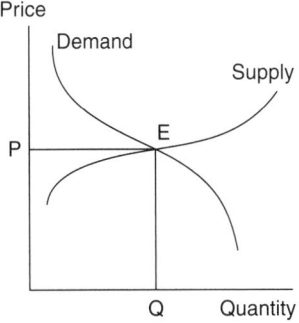

9. Equilibrium of supply and demand

exceed Q along the rising supply curve, and the quantity that consumers demand will be less than Q along the downward-sloping demand curve. Therefore at this high price there will be an excess of supply over demand. Then producers will accept a lower price, and consumers will respond to the lower price. The opposite chain of events will unfold if the price is less than P. Thus from either direction the price will move toward P.

The trouble with this answer is that in the logic of supply and demand curves each consumer and producer responds to 'the prevailing price,' which is outside the control of any one of them. Who, then, adjusts the price toward equilibrium?

Some financial and commodity markets do have explicit market-makers who set the price. Market-makers maintain an inventory of certain assets or commodities, from which they sell to buyers and to which they add what they acquire from sellers. If they see their inventory shrinking, they raise the price; if it is growing they lower the price. Thus the price adjusts to equate the flow into and out of inventory, thereby equating supply and demand. The incentive for market-makers comes from a spread between their buying and selling prices, but in a 'thick' market, in other words one where the volume and number of transactions is large, the spread is small and the outcome is close to the story of the intersection of supply and demand curves.

Most markets lack market-makers; then the processes of matching buyers and sellers and setting prices are more complex and differ from one situation to another. Whether the outcome can be described and studied *as if* it occurs at the supply–demand intersection is unclear, and can only be decided from experience. In Chapter 6 we will meet some examples of other mechanisms, but for now I focus on supply-and-demand as this is the simplest to explain, as well as the source of most common beliefs about markets, some valid and others not.

Efficiency

Figure 10 shows a supply–demand graph; each curve is drawn as a straight line purely for visual simplicity. Imagine the resulting equilibrium at price P and quantity Q as arising from successive decisions to increase quantity starting at zero. The buyer of the very first unit is willing to pay the price indicated by the height A, but only has to pay P. Therefore this buyer derives an extra benefit (the technical term in the jargon of economics is *consumer surplus*) equal to the height AP. The first unit is produced at marginal cost B, but the producer gets price P for it, thus deriving an extra benefit (*producer surplus*) equal to the height BP. Adding the two, the first unit of quantity yields an extra benefit to the economy as a whole (*social surplus*) equal to the height AB.

Proceeding to successively higher quantities, the willingness to pay falls and the marginal cost rises. For the unit of quantity at X, the buyer is willing to pay C and gets consumer surplus CY; the producer incurs marginal cost D and gets producer surplus YD. Therefore this unit of quantity contributes social surplus CY + YD = CD. Finally, at the quantity Q, the buyer pays what he or she is willing to pay, and the producer recoups his or her marginal cost; each gets zero surplus.

For any quantity beyond Q, the buyer's willingness to pay (measured along the falling demand curve) would be less than the producer's marginal cost (measured along the rising supply curve). Such a unit would contribute negative social surplus; it would be inefficient to produce it.

In other words, the supply–demand mechanism produces just the quantity that contributes positive social surplus, and no more. The outcome maximizes the total social surplus; it is economically efficient.

This property of efficiency of markets can be validated in far more general contexts, and constitutes a basic 'theorem' of economics. Of course conclusions of any theorem are valid only so far as its underlying assumptions are valid, and I will have more to say on this. Begin with clarification of the concept of efficiency.

Most importantly, the concept says nothing about how the maximized social surplus is divided among people in the economy. In Figure 10, the total consumer surplus is the area

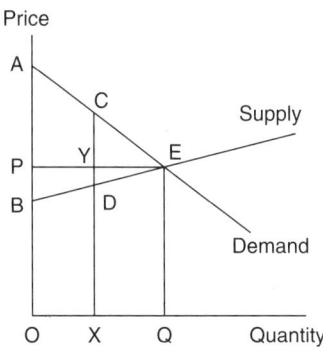

10. Efficiency of supply–demand equilibrium

swept by the heights like AP and CY, namely the area of the triangle APE; the total producer surplus is the area of the triangle BPE. Their relative magnitudes depend on the accidental shapes of demand and supply curves, and say nothing about the merit or justice of the split. Producer surplus contributes to the firms' profit, and goes to their owners as dividends or capital gains. The ethical merit of this is unclear. You may think that owners of firms are always the undeserving rich, but they may include shareholders like your grandparents or parents who get only a modest retirement income from their pension funds.

Economic efficiency of an outcome means merely that any change that benefits one person hurts someone else. It says nothing about distributive justice or ethical merit. The concept is named *Pareto efficiency* for its inventor Vilfredo Pareto, a nineteenth–twentieth-century engineer, sociologist, and economist. To give an extreme example, an outcome is deemed Pareto efficient if any change that benefits a homeless person on the streets of New York hurts Warren Buffett.

Economists' sometimes heartless emphasis on Pareto efficiency has produced some sharp jokes at their expense. My favourite: a businessman, a priest, and an economist are a golf threesome held up by a very slow group ahead of them. After cursing the slowpokes for a long time, they discover that those players are all blind. The businessman is mortified and promises to contribute $10,000 to the Foundation for the Blind. The priest vows to pray to restore their sight. The economist says: 'Wouldn't it promote Pareto efficiency—be better for us, and no worse for them—if they played at night?'

In my opinion efficiency should not be the sole criterion, or in some instances even the primary criterion, to judge economic outcomes; some efficiency should be sacrificed if that yields sufficient improvement in terms of some other social or ethical criterion. I believe Warren Buffett would agree, even though some libertarian or extreme right-wing politicians would not. I said 'should be sacrificed'; whether that happens depends on political institutions and processes.

But wait; the news gets worse. Market outcomes can fail to be efficient even in the limited Pareto sense. When one buyer's or one seller's actions affect others through channels outside the market, adversely as with pollution and congestion and beneficially as with vaccination, market outcomes are not Pareto efficient. And actions to remedy these inefficiencies may be easy for economists to specify on paper but difficult to implement in the real political world. I discuss these issues in the next chapter. Right now let me just warn you against a common pitfall. The word 'equilibrium' misleads people into thinking that everything is for the best in the best of all possible worlds. That is not always or necessarily so: the word merely signifies that the price clears the market; it equates supply and demand. Any other properties, even limited ones like Pareto efficiency, may be valid but must be established separately.

Now for some good news. Many well-meaning policy activists condemn markets using slogans like 'Food for people, not for profit.' Our study of the market mechanism shows that people and profit need not be in conflict. When markets work well (which may need vigilant oversight and regulation), producers' private pursuit of profit efficiently serves the purpose of supplying consumers with their wants for food and other things. High prices signal the wants, and profit provides the incentive to fulfill the wants. In fact this was one of the earliest insights of economics, and was brilliantly expressed by Adam Smith in *The Wealth of Nations*, which is arguably the founding text of economics: 'It is not from the benevolence of the butcher, the brewer, or the baker that we expect our dinner, but from their regard to their own self-interest.'

Shift of equilibrium

If underlying conditions of demand and supply change, market equilibrium will shift from the old intersection to the new one. Whether the price and the quantity increase or decrease depends on the type of shift of demand and supply that has occurred. There are four basic types of such shifts, illustrated in Figure 11. When you have seen and understood these, you will be equipped

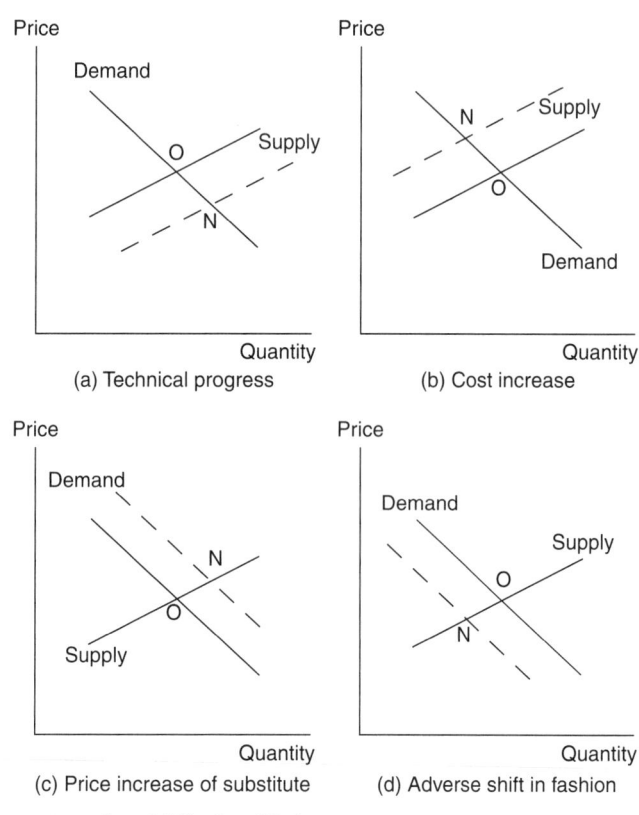

(a) Technical progress

(b) Cost increase

(c) Price increase of substitute

(d) Adverse shift in fashion

11. Examples of shift of equilibrium

to interpret changes in prices and quantities that you observe in many everyday markets.

The figure has four panels, labelled (a)–(d). In each, the original supply and demand curves are shown as solid lines, and one of the curves shifts to a new position shown as a dashed line. (Once again, the curves are shown as straight lines purely for visual simplicity.) The old equilibrium is labelled O and the new one N.

In panel (a), technical progress reduces the cost of production, shifting the supply curve downward. The new equilibrium has lower price and higher quantity than the old one. Flat panel TV sets are the most prominent recent example.

Panel (b) shows the effect of a cost increase, for example the jump in crude oil prices that occurred in 1973 and again in 1979. That increases the marginal cost of producing gasoline, and therefore shifts up its supply curve. The result is an increase in price and a decrease in quantity, as people drive less or switch to more fuel-efficient cars. Of course such responses take time; therefore we should expect the initial impact to be mainly on the price. Gradually as the quantity responds the price will climb back down to some extent. That is exactly what happened in the two episodes of crude oil price shocks.

In panel (c) the source of the shift is an increase in the price of a substitute. Suppose the demand and supply curves shown are those for lager, and the price of ale goes up. Then at any price of lager more of it is bought than before, so the demand curve for lager shifts to the right. The result is more lager sold, and at a higher price as the marginal cost of producing the extra lager goes up.

Panel (d) shows an adverse shift of demand, for example a shift of fashion away from a type of dress. This reduces the quantity and also the price, as the marginal cost goes down along the supply curve.

Consider the fashion shift case a little further. In the short-run, production runs are already committed and stocks are in the stores. Therefore supply is less price-responsive (inelastic or steep), and the brunt of the shift is on price as stores hold clearance sales. Gradually producers shift their lines to producing other now-fashionable garments, the supply curve becomes more price-responsive (elastic or flat), and the main effect is a decrease in quantity of the now unfashionable item. Figure 12 shows these cases separately; the new equilibrium is labelled S in the short-run panel on the left and L in the long-run panel on the right.

Thus price and quantity may each rise or fall by a little or a lot depending on the circumstances. You have probably seen all combinations at different times in different markets, and wondered why price and quantity move together at some times and not others, and why sometimes price changes a lot and sometimes it is the quantity that changes. Now you can understand each episode by thinking about an underlying cause that shifts the supply curve upwards or downwards, or the demand curve to the right or to the left, and the length of time over which the equilibrium adjusts.

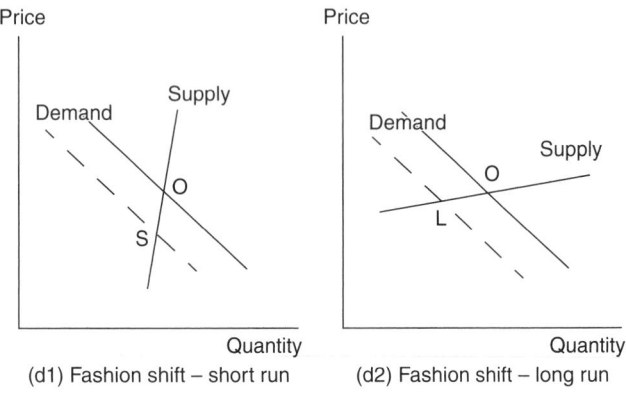

12. Effect of fashion shift in the short- and long-runs

Taxes

One cause of equilibrium shift merits special attention: imposition of a tax. As the simplest example, consider a tax of a specified amount per unit of quantity. Suppose the seller is required to keep records and pay the tax to the government. Then the seller's tax-inclusive marginal cost rises by the amount of the tax, and the supply curve rises vertically. Figure 13 shows the result. The new equilibrium is at N, and the price buyers pay is given by the height of B. Of this, the government gets the tax, which equals the height of the shift of the supply curve and therefore equals BS. Sellers get only the price given by the height of S. Before the tax was imposed, buyers paid and sellers received the same price, namely the height of P. The tax has raised the price buyers pay from P to B, and lowered the price sellers receive from P to S. We can say that of the total tax BS, buyers pay BP and sellers pay PS. These effects are called the *incidence* of the tax.

Even though the sellers hand over the tax to the government, buyers end up paying part of it through the higher price. In fact,

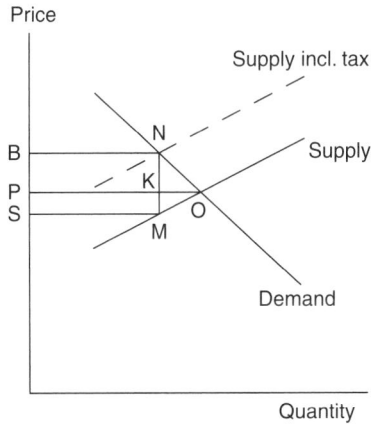

13. Effect of a tax

who initially pays the tax is irrelevant; as the effects of the tax work their way through the market equilibrium, the eventual incidence is the same. There may be only transitory differences as the market moves to its new equilibrium.

This point is often not understood. Consider the US social security tax. Formally, employers pay a part of it, and workers pay the rest. But this eventually works its way through the labour market with the same consequence for wages as when one side initially pays all the tax. The policy debates we see frequently about whether it is unfair to ask workers to pay part of the tax, or whether taxing employers will be bad for employment, are mostly immaterial.

The tax reduces the quantity traded in the market; the new equilibrium N has a smaller quantity than the old equilibrium O. Quantities between N and O could have been traded to the mutual benefit of the buyers and sellers: absent the tax, buyers are willing to pay more than the sellers' marginal cost. The tax creates inefficiency: total surplus equal to the area of the triangle NMO is lost, of which NKO is consumer surplus and KMO producer surplus. But these efficiency losses should not automatically condemn the tax: if the revenue it raises serves some socially useful purpose, that benefit can outweigh the loss.

Subsidies have similar incidence effects. Deductibility of mortgage interest in the US and many other countries is such a subsidy, usually justified as a policy to spread benefits of homeownership to the masses. Figure 14 shows its effects under different conditions of supply in the housing market. In both panels the subsidy raises the demand curve for housing: anyone who was willing to pay x for a house before is now willing to pay x plus the subsidy because the government is picking up the subsidy part leaving the individual to pay the same x as before. The equilibrium shifts from the old O to the new M. The nature of the shift depends very much on the conditions of supply. In the left-hand panel the supply is unresponsive to price (inelastic); that is so in

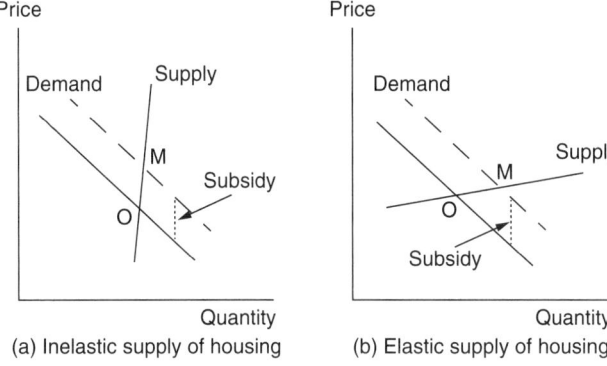

(a) Inelastic supply of housing   (b) Elastic supply of housing

14. Incidence of mortgage interest deductibility

the short-run, and can be so even in the long-run if local government regulations restrict new construction. The price rise from O to M is almost equal to the subsidy and the quantity increase is small: the subsidy gets almost entirely swallowed up in price increases of existing housing with little expansion of home-ownership. Existing homeowners are the main beneficiaries; no wonder the deduction is politically so popular. New buyers willing to pay the higher price are mostly rich; spreading homeownership to them is not the stated intention of the policy. In the right-hand panel supply is price-responsive (elastic); here the quantity increases and the price rises only a little, which is more in keeping with the intent. But for this to happen, the government should not restrict construction of new housing by zoning or other regulations.

The budget deficits and debt accumulation of governments in the United States and elsewhere has led them to think of eliminating or restricting the mortgage interest deduction from their income tax laws. You can run the above analysis backwards and see that such a reform will mainly hurt existing homeowners, at least in the short-run. That explains the strong political opposition to these proposals.

Cycles of booms and busts

As I mentioned earlier and re-emphasize now, most markets do not have market-makers to equate demand and supply and keep the market continuously in equilibrium. There may still be tendencies toward equilibrium. For example, if a price is too high, there is excess supply and some producers are unable to sell. They will eventually resort to clearance sales to attract buyers, so prices will fall. However, this may be a slow process. In other situations, adjustments may be too rapid, leading to cycles of prices shooting above and below the equilibrium level. Here are a couple of examples.

In some markets, such as housing and commodity mining, supply is fixed in the short-run but responds to prices with a time delay. Before that happens, price is determined so as to equate demand and the available fixed supply. The left-hand panel of Figure 15 shows what can then happen. Suppose initially the price is too low, and the supply responds to put the market at the point labelled 1. Pressure of demand raises the price, moving the market to the point 2. After some delay supply responds to this higher price, taking us to the point 3. To absorb this excess supply, the

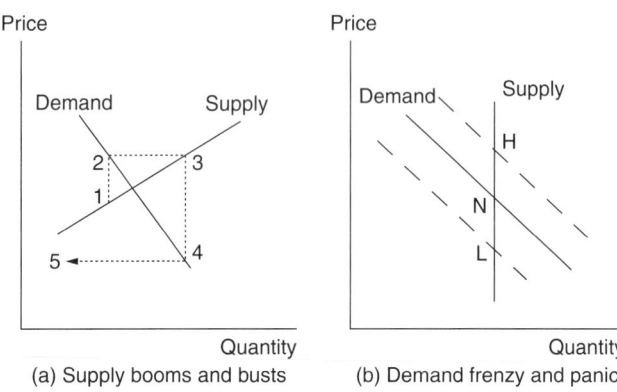

(a) Supply booms and busts   (b) Demand frenzy and panic

15. Price fluctuations

price must drop, resulting in the point 4. And so on. The demand and supply curves shown are such that this process is actually unstable; with other shapes the cycles could gradually dampen down but disequilibrium may persist for a long time.

One would think that over time producers would understand the nature of the price fluctuations—look further into the future and not respond to the last price observed. But that does not seem to happen; we do observe such fluctuations and even instabilities in housing and mining.

The right-hand panel of Figure 14 shows price fluctuations that occur in many financial markets when demand chases the trend. Without such behaviour by investors, equilibrium would be at N (for normal). But suppose the price rises a little above N for some accidental reason. Investors interpret this as a trend; they expect the price will rise even higher and they will profit if they buy now. Demand shifts up and price rises to a point like the one labelled H. This may create even more pressure of demand—you could call this greed or frenzy. Eventually new buyers are scarce; the price rises slowly or even falls a little. This sets up the opposite reaction—which you could call fear or panic. That shifts demand downwards and price collapses to a point like L. Once again, if investors understood the whole process they might not be moved to such extreme reactions, but individuals and even markets collectively have short memories, and every few years we see alternating booms and busts.

Price floors and ceilings

Sometimes governments keep markets away from equilibrium by imposing upper or lower limits on prices. The motive may be to benefit some politically favoured special interests at the expense of others, or it may be to address some need or want that is deemed socially more important or urgent enough. (Or it may be the first motive masquerading as the second!) In both cases, the policies have side-effects that are often harmful, sometimes even to the intended beneficiaries.

The European Union's (EU) Common Agricultural Policy aims 'to ensure a fair standard of living for farmers and to provide a stable and safe food supply at affordable prices for consumers'. For almost five decades the EU pursued these lofty goals by stipulating minimum prices for various farm products. The left-hand panel of Figure 16 shows the result. At the price P, producers wish to supply the quantity corresponding to the point labelled B while consumers demand only the quantity A. Suppliers could have been restricted, but the EU usually allowed and purchased the excess supply AB. The media gave these surpluses colourful names like the 'butter mountain' and the 'wine lake'. Some of the surpluses were sold at very low prices to countries outside the EU; the loss incurred by paying farmers high prices and reselling at low prices was borne by EU taxpayers. Countries with large farming populations were net beneficiaries; the more industrialized member countries were net losers. This created much political conflict in the EU. Recently the policy has been reformed to give farmers direct income support not linked to their production. That has

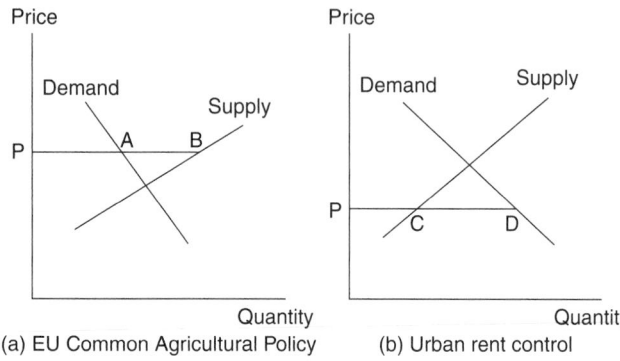

(a) EU Common Agricultural Policy   (b) Urban rent control

16. Price floors and ceilings

eliminated the surpluses, but conflicts arising from different allocation of benefits and costs across countries remain.

From the 1930s to the 1980s the US had a similar policy of dairy price supports. The result: an abandoned mine full of cheese growing mouldy, accumulated at a cost of $4 billion per year, and maintained at a cost of $1 million per day.

As cities grow, the pressure of demand shows up in rising rents. Incumbent tenants dislike having to pay more. Some city governments respond by imposing rent controls. New York after World War II was a prime example but there are others; you may have lived in one and experienced the consequences. The right-hand panel of Figure 16 shows the direct effect. With price not allowed to rise above the point P, demand is at D and supply at C, creating excess demand equal to DC. That sets in motion a whole chain of events, most of them inefficient or even pernicious. Landlords or their agents engage in favouritism or discrimination when renting, or extract payments like 'key money' from prospective renters. People sublet rooms, often illegally, causing overcrowding. Landlords provide poor services and skip maintenance, so the controlled rent eventually gets renters a low quality of housing. Builders find new construction unprofitable at the controlled rents; this aggravates the scarcity over time. The city government responds by relieving new construction from rent control, but that precludes efficient allocation of space. For example an old couple who raised their family in a large rent-controlled apartment would now like to move into a smaller new one but cannot do so because the rent there is much higher; in the meantime a young family that needs a large apartment cannot find one. In extreme cases these side-effects may wipe out the benefits of even the intended beneficiaries of the policy, namely the original occupiers. But the policy persists, because politicians fear the immediate impact of any repeal: rents of the controlled apartments will rise, creating adverse media coverage and a political backlash.

Here we have examples of policies that may have started out with good intentions—to ensure decent incomes for farmers and affordable housing for city-dwellers—but ended up creating very costly side-effects and in the long-run sometimes hurting even the intended beneficiaries. In the next chapter we will see more examples of market failures and policy failures alike, leading me to conclude that perfection is unattainable and that we must accept the least imperfect among feasible solutions to economic problems, mixing market-based and governmental solutions as appropriate for each problem.

Chapter 5
Market and policy failures

Monopoly and oligopoly

The efficient outcome at the intersection of the demand and supply curves requires price to be outside the control of any one producer. If a firm is large enough to influence the market price, it can profit by curtailing supply to drive up the price along the demand curve. Several firms may be able to collude and achieve the same result. Exactly how much the supply is curtailed will depend on the context, and the details of that analysis are not important in this brief introduction. But the consequences are.

Figure 17 reproduces Figure 10 with some modification. Suppose monopoly or oligopoly reduces quantity to a point such as X, less than Q. Then the social surplus contributed by quantities between X and Q, namely the excess of the willingness to pay over the marginal cost of these quantities, amounting to the area CDE, is lost. This measures the inefficiency of the monopoly or oligopoly (the technical term is *dead-weight loss*).

If all the buyers of the quantity X pay the same price, namely C along the demand curve, then an amount equal to the area of the rectangle MCYP, which would have been part of the consumer surplus under perfect competition, now becomes a part of the firms' profits. Any successful price discrimination

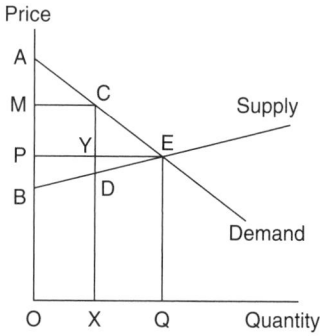

17. Inefficiency of monopoly

can extract even more surplus from the consumers. This raises the possibility that firms may expend resources to facilitate acquisition of monopoly power—deter entry of competitors, pay political contributions or even bribes to obtain and sustain their monopoly power, sometimes in the guise of 'national champions'. These resource expenditures also do not contribute to overall social welfare, and must count as inefficiencies.

How big are the effects of monopoly power? Hospital treatment in the US provides an extreme example. Patients have few or no competing alternatives in their area, they lack information about prices and cost-effective treatments, and they have neither time nor ability to make rational choices in urgent or emergency situations. And rationally calculating patients with good insurance coverage are undeterred by high prices. Therefore providers can charge prices ten or more times costs. For example, the maker of a spinal stimulation device that cost about $4,500 to produce sold it to a hospital for about $19,000, which then charged the patient $49,237 for it! (That did not include the doctors' and hospital's charges for installing it; the total bill for a day's outpatient procedure was $86,951.) As a general principle, the less price-responsive the demand, the greater the potential to raise price above cost.

What about economy-wide efficiency losses due to monopoly and oligopoly? Estimates for the US vary from 0.1 per cent to 7 per cent of gross domestic product (GDP); in countries where antitrust laws and their enforcement are less stringent, the fraction may be higher. Even 1 per cent of GDP is sizeable: in the US this is about \$150 billion per year, or \$500 per US citizen. Seen from another angle, a 2 per cent drop in GDP is similar to the average for recessions in the years 1947–2006; the Great Recession of 2007–9 had a GDP drop of about 5 per cent. But the loss due to monopoly occurs every year, not just one–two years out of every four–five as with recessions. Thus inefficiency of monopoly is a problem of magnitude comparable to that of recessions in macroeconomics. Effective antitrust policy is correspondingly important, but the political process may be captured by existing and would-be monopolists, as pointed out above.

Might some monopoly power be necessary for innovation and growth? Both theory and evidence are unclear on this point. The prospect of temporary monopoly profits resulting from a new idea or product, whether protected by a patent or simply because other firms need time to imitate and produce rival products, might spur research and development. Profits from previous monopoly power might also generate internal financing for these activities. But a secure monopoly may blunt the incentive to innovate; firms may hesitate to develop new products that cannibalize the market for their own existing products. In my opinion the most important thing is to preserve freedom of entry into markets. Then entrepreneurs with new ideas and products can put them to the test of consumer acceptance, and incumbent firms will also continue to innovate for fear of losing out to some newcomer.

Externalities, negative, and positive

Many actions of consumers or firms have side-effects, beneficial or harmful to others. When you drive your car you pollute the air, which harms other people's health, and you add to congestion on the roads, which increases others' driving time. When you get vaccinated, you reduce not only your own risk of catching the disease, but also that of passing it on to others. If you keep your front yard beautiful, you increase the pleasure of your neighbours and passers-by. Toxic discharges and greenhouse gas emissions of mining companies and power plants can harm people's health and perhaps endanger the future of human life on earth.

In many such situations, people and firms lack the incentives to take into account the by-product effects when making their choices. Alas, most of us are not sufficiently other-regarding to include the harm or benefit to others automatically in our calculations. When we ignore the harm our action imposes on others, we carry the action beyond the level that would be best for aggregate social efficiency; when we ignore the benefits to others, we do too little. That is why we see too much congestion on our roads, and sometimes dangerously low vaccination coverage of the population. Economists call such effects *externalities*, positive when they are beneficial to others and negative when they are harmful.

It is important to emphasize that not every good or bad by-product of an action is an externality. When you buy something, you use up the labour, materials, and other resources that went into making it, leaving less for others. But the price you pay for your purchase in a well-functioning competitive market equals the marginal cost of production. Therefore you face the correct scarcity price of your action, and have the correct incentive to economize on the use of society's scarce resources. Only when you do not face the correct scarcity price, as in cases like clean air and roads, will your actions create externalities. What is an externality therefore depends on whether a market puts the correct price on that action. Unfortunately many such markets are missing or malfunctioning, and externalities are ubiquitous.

What is the total social cost of externalities? They arise in too many and too varied contexts to allow calculation of a reliable overall number, but an important instance will serve to illustrate the magnitude of the problem. In their 1994 *American Scientist* article, Richard Arnott and Kenneth Small calculated that, in the US, traffic congestion caused delays of 6 billion vehicle hours. Assuming the average number of people was 1.5 per vehicle, and valuing the average person's time at $12 an hour (the average wage that year), the cost of traffic congestion was $108 billion. It has surely risen since. Other instances can be even more costly. If the effects of global climate change prove as bad as some fear, the externality costs of carbon emissions could be huge.

How can these inefficiencies be remedied? Two approaches exist: one market-based the other government-based. Each has its merits and drawbacks—which works better depends on the context. Neither is ever perfect, but separately and together they offer significant improvement over doing nothing.

We have seen how prices create incentives to produce goods and services that someone is willing to pay for, and to economize on consumption of high-priced goods and services. The market-based approach applies these insights to things like clean air or toxic waste, for which no market or price would otherwise exist.

For a market to operate, what is being transacted must be clearly defined, and someone must have an 'alienable' right to it: a right that can be sold to someone else. Suppose society awards all citizens a right to clean air. Then a firm that pollutes the air as a by-product of its activities must buy the right from them. It is willing to pay a price up to the extra profit that activity will generate. For a price, the citizens may be willing to sell the right, if in their judgement the money they get is worth more than the damage from pollution they will suffer. If the price the firm is willing to pay exceeds the total that the citizens demand, the two sides have the basis for a trade. By making both sides better off (each by its own judgement) the trade promotes Pareto efficiency.

Alternatively, firms can be given rights to pollute, and allowed to make enforceable contracts with citizens promising not to pollute in exchange for a price. That also increases efficiency (to reinforce your understanding, I recommend that you do the reasoning for this case). Distribution of the efficiency gains differs in the two cases: each side is better off when it has the right than when the other has it.

If such markets can be established and function well, prices will exist and will convey information and incentives efficiently in the usual way. For example, if clean air is very scarce, citizens will demand a high price to allow pollution; if firms have to pay this price in order to pollute, they have strong incentives to use or develop less-polluting technologies. This is the motivation behind markets for carbon emission trading that exist, for example, in Europe and California.

Unfortunately, well-functioning markets of this kind are difficult to create and operate. Perhaps the greatest difficulty in the emissions market is that clean air is a collective good, in contrast to a private good like bread of which each buyer consumes what he or she buys. The same air affects everyone in a locality, and carbon emissions may affect everyone on earth. The market has to find out what price every affected person is willing to accept for allowing more emissions, and add this up over them all. People can game this system. Each thinks that if he or she overstates the price it will make very little difference to the outcome; when they all do so, the total price gets so high that firms are not willing to pay it and the market collapses. Worse, in the case of long-lived pollution and emissions that can cause permanent damage like global warming, the future generations who will be adversely affected are unable to participate in today's market. Other difficulties arise in other contexts. More generally, Ronald Coase's insight that markets have transaction costs is valid here just as it was in the discussion of firms' decisions to make or buy, which I discussed in Chapter 3.

Indeed, Coase himself developed this idea in his pioneering analysis of the market approach for coping with externalities. He argued that *if* there were no transaction costs, markets would yield efficient solutions without any need for government intervention (except in its usual roles of defining and enforcing property rights and enforcing voluntary private contracts). This has subsequently often been misunderstood: the big *if* at the opening of Coase's argument is often forgotten, and the implication—efficient markets—is wrongly thought to be a universal rule.

Among small stable groups where actions are easy to monitor and enforce using long-term relationships and reputations, Coasian efficient outcomes can be sustained without top–down governance. Indeed, the local information available to insiders makes bottom–up group action superior. Consider the benefit homeowners provide to their neighbours by keeping their houses and gardens beautiful. Condominium associations can handle this perfectly well by devising norms and sanctions; even informal social pressure to conform to a neighbourhood's norm can have the right effect. A government bureaucrat would find it very difficult to elicit a group's tastes in these matters and devise and enforce appropriate laws.

Elinor Ostrom demonstrated the potential and limits of bottom–up collective action in her Nobel-prize-winning research of original case studies and meta-analysis of other studies. Fisheries are a good example. Each person's fishing reduces what is available to others. This negative externality can lead to overfishing or even extinction of the stock, to the detriment of all.

The fishermen are all aware of the problem, but each of them has only a negligible effect on the risk of extinction and they personally benefit by fishing more. Thus they are trapped in a prisoner's dilemma. Small stable groups, for example a lake-fishing community, can draw up rules for the size and allocation of the catch, and enforce these by using threats of punishment including social ostracism. But it is harder for ocean fisheries to do this, as fish migrate far and the fishermen come from many localities and countries. Overfishing has indeed endangered or made extinct populations of Atlantic cod, Chilean sea bass, Bluefin tuna, and other ocean fish species.

Sometimes the Coasian solution can work beyond small, tight social groups. A beekeeper benefits orchard-owners by providing pollination services. This was one of the earliest examples of a positive externality mentioned in economics. In reality private arrangements resolve it very well: beekeepers hire their services to orchard owners. This goes beyond local deals; beekeepers maintain mobile hives on trucks, and travel from south to north following the flowering seasons in different regions.

Next consider government-based approaches. These can include incentives with effects similar to those of prices, namely taxes or subsidies. Such policies are called Pigouvian after Arthur Pigou, a twentieth-century British economist who pioneered their analysis. A tax on carbon emissions increases firms' incentives to use clean technologies; a subsidy for solar or wind power generation increases the incentive for power companies to use more of those methods.

The tax or subsidy for an action should equal the by-product damage or benefit the action confers on others. For a quick illustration to understand this, observe that car drivers' violations of traffic laws are monitored more carefully and punished more severely than pedestrians' violations of jaywalking laws. This makes good sense: a car driver's mistake creates a much bigger negative externality than that of a pedestrian.

Costs of externalities can be difficult to assess. Objective measurements are often not feasible. Asking the parties may not yield honest answers. If the government compensates people and firms for harm they suffer from pollution created by others, they may overstate their harm; if it taxes or fines them for toxic discharges, they may attempt to evade the tax by diverting the discharges into other even more harmful outlets. Prospects are better if the needed information is purely statistical, pertaining to the aggregate of the population and not to individuals or particular firms, because then it can be obtained by anonymous sample surveys (provided people believe that their anonymity will be respected!).

Modern technology has made it easier to gather the needed information in some cases. For example, many cities now impose tolls on cars to access their congested centres, using cameras placed all around the periphery of the central areas to photograph licence plates of entering cars and send bills to the owners, or by using more advanced transponder devices placed in the cars. These charges can be varied according to the time of day, or even the actual level of congestion continuously monitored by cameras placed at many locations in the city centres.

Governments can also attempt quantity controls—restrictions or bans on emissions, requirements of minimum fuel efficiency for cars, and so on. But such policies require information that is not usually directly available to the government agencies that promulgate and enforce the controls, and firms lack the incentives to supply honest information. For example, suppose a limit on the country's total emissions has been decided, and it remains to allocate this quota among firms. A firm that does not have a permit has to find other ways to reduce or eliminate its emissions, and this is costly. Therefore it is efficient to give emission quotas to the firms whose cost of abating emissions is highest. Then each firm wants to overstate its costs in order to win more permits. It would be better to use a market-like solution that makes firms put their money where their mouths are: auction the quotas, so firms that find it hardest to do without will bid most for the quotas.

Determination of the aggregate quotas is also difficult and often becomes politicized. Indeed, the European Union's carbon emission trading market is beset by such problems. Too many permits were awarded, the price collapsed, and the scheme has lost much of its purpose.

To sum up, each of the approaches—Coasian market-based and Pigouvian government-based—has its problems. Luckily the two have different problems. The Coasian approach works better in small and stable groups; the Pigouvian one works better in large populations when anonymous statistical information can be used. Even then government policies are likely to work better if they have market-like features, for example auctioning emission quotas instead of awarding them by a bureaucratic process. In some instances a mixture of the two approaches may work best; for example, quotas that are auctioned but can be traded in secondary markets. Shifting equilibrium in these markets preserves efficiency as conditions change over time. Even jointly the two methods will not resolve all externalities perfectly, but nothing is perfect and we must accept the least imperfect solution that is available.

An example will help you remember the relative merits of the two methods. I apologize for its impropriety, but that is what makes it memorable. If you are more skilled at sex, your partner gets more pleasure from the act. How should this externality be handled? In monogamous societies, couples can achieve the Coasian optimum by private agreement. But in promiscuous societies, the government can do better by giving Pigouvian subsidies to education in 'marital arts'!

Information asymmetries

An important, but often unstated, requirement for a market to function well is that the parties to the transaction should have a clear idea of what they are buying or selling. But in many instances one party is much better informed than the other: sellers know product quality better than do buyers, and buyers of insurance policies know their own risks better than do the companies that issue the policies. Strategies to interpret, elicit, conceal, or reveal information play key roles in such interactions, and affect market outcomes.

George Akerlof's Nobel-prize-winning analysis of the market for lemons (cars with serious defects) dramatically alerted economists to such effects, including the possibility of a complete collapse of the market. I mentioned this briefly in Chapter 1; here is a fuller outline.

Consider the following scenario. Each car can be either peach-perfect, worth $15,000 if its quality could be credibly guaranteed, or a worthless lemon. In the total population of cars, 2/3 are peaches and 1/3 are lemons. Each seller knows the type of his or her own car, but prospective buyers cannot know the quality of any individual car. Buyers are willing to pay what they believe to be the average value of cars on the market.

Could the market price be 2/3 * $15,000 + 1/3 * $0 = $10,000? Yes, if cars on the market were a representative sample of the population. But they are not. A seller who knows his or her car to be a peach is reluctant to sell it for $10,000. Some may sell because they are moving, are in financial trouble, or for some such reason. Just to be definite, suppose half of peach owners are willing to sell for $10,000. All lemon owners are of course glad to get this price. Therefore the mix of cars on the market consists of the 1/3 of the population that are lemons, and half of the 2/3rd that are peaches. The market is an equal mix of peaches and lemons, so the value of the average car is only 1/2 * $15,000 + 1/2 * $0 = $7,500.

But that is not the end of the story. At this lower price, even more peach owners drop out of the market: the movers may decide to take their car, or those in financial trouble persuade their relatives to help. Suppose only 1/4 of peaches remain. Now the market consists of the 1/3 of the population of cars that are lemons, and 1/4 of 2/3rds, that is 1/6, that are peaches. This is a 2:1 mix of lemons and peaches: of the used cars on the market, 1/3 are peaches and 2/3 are lemons. So the average value drops to 1/3 * $15,000 + 2/3 * $0 = $5,000.

The process could go on until all peach-owners drop out and only lemons remain on the used car market. But even short of such complete market collapse, the used car market becomes an unrepresentative sample of the population of cars; lemons are overrepresented and peaches are rare.

Although dramatic, is a market collapse realistic? Anyone who has bought a used car knows that the process is fraught with uncertainty and worry about quality. But a market exists, and high-quality used cars are traded. Owners of good used cars have ways of giving credible assurances to buyers.

Reputation is an important device of this kind. In the private market, if the seller is a friend, or a friend of a friend, or even a friend three or four steps removed in a chain, the seller wants to remain in the good books of the whole friendship network, and is more likely to be forthcoming about any known defects in the car. A warranty would be a good device, but the buyer can't be sure that the seller will be available and will fulfill the warranty if and when this is needed, so it ultimately relies on the reputation of the seller.

What about professional dealers? Used car dealers may make a quick buck by cheating a few customers, but their bad reputation will spread and they won't last long in the business. But how do you know whether the dealer you are negotiating with is in the business for the long haul or a fly-by-nighter? You look for evidence of stability. Does the dealer simultaneously sell new cars of an established brand? Has the dealership been at the location for a while? Do the premises convey an aura of permanence or do they look as if everything could be dismantled and the storefront converted into a restaurant in a couple of days? Such indicators of stability are costly; an unpaved parking lot and a hut for an office would be a lot cheaper than a fancy storefront and well-maintained car lot. It is precisely this cost that makes the indicators credible. A dealer who means to be in the business for a long time can amortize the cost over many years and so can afford it; a fly-by-nighter cannot. The same principle also helps explain why banks have large and impressive premises; they are proclaiming, 'We are here to stay, so your money is safe with us.'

Michael Spence developed this idea of costly signals in work that won him a Nobel prize jointly with Akerlof and Joseph Stiglitz; these three launched the whole field of the economics of asymmetric information. Spence's theory is best explained in the labour market. Imagine yourself interviewing for a job. The conversation goes as follows:

EMPLOYER:	This job requires high quantitative skills and strong work ethic.
YOU:	Sure, I have plenty of both of these.
EMPLOYER:	Why should I believe you? Anyone can say that.
YOU:	Look at my college transcript. I took tough maths, statistics, and economics courses, and got As. That requires not only first-rate quantitative skills, but also the willpower to work every night completing all problem set assignments.
EMPLOYER:	Wouldn't everyone do the same to qualify for this high-paying job?

YOU: No. A non-quantitative student couldn't handle the work; one lacking true dedication would succumb to the temptations of campus social life.

Words are cheap; the employer wants you to 'put your money where your mouth is', so to speak. You offer your educational achievement as a *signal* that you have the qualities the employer wants. The signal is costly: you have to spend time and effort and resist temptations in order to acquire the signal. But more than that: the cost of the signal—in terms of time, effort, and giving up campus parties—would be prohibitively high to someone who lacked the qualities you are signalling. It is this *cost difference*—you, with the right qualities, can afford the cost of the signal but someone without them cannot—that distinguishes you from a would-be mimic or pretender and makes credible your assertion of quality.

Signals can thus solve the asymmetric information problem, but at a cost. Who pays this cost depends on the context. In the education example, those who lack the quantitative skills and the work ethic would like to get the high-paying jobs (at least for a year or so until they are found out and thrown out), and will mimic the actions of the truly skilled, unless the bar is set high enough. The hurdle must usually exceed the level of education that genuinely improves your productivity on the job. The innately skilled and dedicated must therefore spend some time and effort in getting education that is productively wasteful, solely for its signalling purpose. The mere existence of dummies and slackers creates a cost for the better students to prove credibly that they are not dummies or slackers!

We can relate this to the discussion of externalities in the previous section. The dummies and slackers, by their mere existence, are imposing a negative externality on the skilled and dedicated, who must invest excessively in education in order to prove that they are not one of the undesirable types.

Indeed, many effects of information asymmetries can be seen through the lens of externalities, and the market failures resulting from these externalities can be remedied, albeit only imperfectly, by Coasian or Pigouvian methods as appropriate. I will discuss and illustrate this approach in the concluding section of this chapter.

The screening devices for price discrimination we met in Chapter 3 are a mirror-image of signalling. Firms comprise the less informed side of the interaction, and choose pricing strategies to separate and attract those buyer types that yield them the most profit while discouraging the rest. Signalling is initiated by the informed side, but in many cases could instead be implemented as screening by the uninformed side. In the education example, employers can (and often do) stipulate qualifications tough enough that only the truly skilled and dedicated workers will achieve them; then they are screening applicants instead of the applicants signalling to them.

Once you understand the concept, you start to see signalling and screening everywhere, not only or primarily in markets, but in all kinds of social interactions. Here is a tiny sample.

Mafias have initiation rites that require new recruits to perform specified criminal deeds, often murders. These serve as measures of the requisite toughness and ruthlessness, but they are also effective devices to screen out police infiltrators or investigative reporters: someone like that might comply if the test was merely one of toughness, but not if it requires criminal acts.

The theory of sexual selection in evolutionary biology says that females choose mates with special attention to genetic superiority, because given their limited number of breeding opportunities, they must seek to maximize the fitness of each offspring. The large antlers of stags, or the heavy and elaborate plumage of peacocks and birds of paradise, are a handicap to carry and defend.

Therefore they serve as credible signals of genetic quality: only an exceptionally fit male can afford the resources needed to develop and maintain these features.

Finally an example from ordinary life. You are on a first date with someone you find attractive. You know you won't get a second chance to make a good first impression. But you also know that your date will watch out for fake first impressions. In other words, you are signalling and your date is screening. If the date finds you attractive, there may be traffic in the other direction too. What are good signals in this context, and what are good screening devices? Both are likely to be situation-specific, so I leave you to think what can work in your context. I only emphasize the importance of careful thinking. It is too easy to lose a lifetime's happiness by being unaware of the information game that is going on: failing to give a credible signal or failing to screen effectively.

Moral hazard and adverse selection

Two important types of information asymmetries can be illustrated using insurance markets. People can mitigate many health risks by diet and exercise. An insurance contract may specify that the insured is required to do this, but the company can only very imperfectly monitor adherence by the insured. People may then be tempted to shirk exercising or order the calorie-laden dessert; to some extent the temptation may be greater in the knowledge that they have insurance to cover their medical expenses. Insurance companies of course regard such behaviour as immoral. That industry coined the term *moral hazard* for such situations; it has now become standard economic usage for situations of transactions where one party's actions are not observable to the other party, or not demonstrable to a third party that may be called upon to enforce the contract.

The insured may also have better knowledge of their own innate risks than does the insurance company. Then any given insurance contract is most attractive to the worst risks, and the company selectively attracts them to its offering. This is called *adverse selection*. Again the term is used more generally for situations where one party to a transaction knows some relevant attribute better than does the other. Akerlof's market for lemons is a great example. Current owners of used cars know their quality better than do prospective buyers; therefore at any price the market attracts sellers of relatively low quality cars.

We saw how the used car market can potentially fail. A similar problem can arise with health care. The Affordable Care Act in the United States (the so-called 'Obamacare') makes coverage available at a stated price to all applicants. Older and relatively unhealthy people are more likely to want the coverage; the young and healthy may choose to stay uninsured, even if they have to pay the small fine that the law imposes for this. The insurance pool thus adversely selects the worst health risks; premiums must be high enough to cover their costs if the policies are to be financially self-sufficient.

Informationally disadvantaged parties in transactions have various ways of coping with their disadvantage. The screening devices we saw in the previous section are ways of coping with adverse selection. Moral hazard in insurance can be mitigated by providing incomplete insurance using deductibles and co-pays; this leaves the insured facing some risk, and giving them some incentive to expend care to reduce the risk. Moral hazard in the workplace can be reduced by making the employee's compensation depend on observable consequences of his or her actions. For example, if output or profit is observable to the employer and is affected at least in part by the quality or quantity of the employee's effort, then output-based payments or profit-sharing will mitigate moral hazard. But none of these devices can achieve an outcome as efficient as the hypothetical possibility with full and symmetric information. The inefficiency that remains is akin to an externality; I will illustrate this later in this chapter using examples from the recent financial crisis.

Profit externalities between firms

One firm's actions affect demand for substitutes and complements to its products, and therefore profits of firms selling those products. Such interactions have implications for market structures and therefore economic consequences to the consumers of these products.

Suppose coffee and tea (a pair of substitutes) are made and sold by different firms, each with some market power. Let us call the firms Java and Assam, respectively. If Java raises the price of coffee, demand shifts toward tea (for a reminder, see Figure 3 in Chapter 2 and the associated text). With a stronger demand for tea, Assam can raise its price and make more profit. This is as if Java is bestowing a positive externality on Assam. But Java is not concerned with Assam's profit; it ignores the externality. Therefore it does not raise its price as high as the combined interest of the two firms would warrant. Assam's pricing decision has the same issue. Both firms would do better to merge into one—let us call it Caffeine—which would then raise prices of both products and make more profit than the sum of profits of the separate firms. Of course the higher prices hurt consumers. Thus makers of substitutes have incentives to merge, and antitrust policy should be on guard for any resulting price increases that harm consumers.

Next consider a pair of complements, computer hardware and software, made and sold by firms called Chips and Codes, respectively. If Chips raises the price of its hardware, demand for software declines, hurting Codes' profits. This is a negative externality. In any activity like pollution that has a negative externality, private choices lead to excess. Here Chips pushes its price rise farther than the joint interests of the two firms warrant.

So does Codes. If these two firms merged into one, it would increase total profit by reducing both prices: the lower price of each product sufficiently stimulates demand for the other. The lower prices also benefits consumers. This is a rare win-win-win situation; merger benefits the two firms *and* consumers. Antitrust policy should not prohibit mergers of complements; on the contrary it should encourage them!

A difficult trade-off

Many products have high first-copy costs, and after these have been incurred, the marginal cost of supplying each unit is small. The best examples come from the tech sector. Creation and debugging of software for operating systems, browsers, and major application programs takes many programmers' time over many months and millions of dollars; once the programs are ready, they can be disseminated almost costlessly over the web. The pharmaceutical industry is similar. The cost of research, development, and testing of each new miracle drug is huge, especially since many failed trials lie behind each success. Once the drug is available and approved, the cost of production and delivery is tiny.

How should such products be priced? Consider the situation once they are available and are being marketed. Efficiency at this point requires expanding supply until the willingness to pay for the next unit equals its marginal cost. That would imply a very low price—almost zero for software. Indeed, many idealists advocate exactly this. They say that information can be disseminated to everyone for free (or almost free), so there should be no charge for it. They argue that charging more for a life-saving drug than the tiny cost of making it is morally reprehensible.

But at such low prices the makers of these products will not recoup the high first-copy costs. And if precedents are established for selling existing products at low prices leaving the makers to bear the first-copy costs, that will deter future drug researchers and software developers, which will hurt future consumers too. There is truth to this argument, although sometimes firms disingenuously advance it to justify monopoly prices out of all reasonable proportion to the first-copy costs and the need for incentives.

Social policy therefore faces an unavoidable dilemma or trade-off between promoting new research and development on the one hand, and disseminating the results at low marginal cost on the other. The resolution is a compromise: firms or individuals who develop or create such products are given a monopoly over their sales for a limited period: patents for drugs and other innovations, copyrights for software and books.

Why not pay first-copy costs from general tax revenues and let producers charge only the low (perhaps near-zero) marginal? Such a system would create bad incentives. No one knows in advance whether a new drug will be effective, or a new book worth reading, or a piece of software worth using. Charlatans and politically well-connected people would make a nice living by persuading the authorities to pay them as they wasted time and finally confessed to failure. The tiny number of potential consumers of a rare drug or a highly specialized computer program would agitate to get taxpayer support for their special needs. The patent and copyright system reduces such risks by making developers and consumers put their money where their mouths are. It is not perfect but, once again, nothing is perfect.

Collective goods

When they function well, markets supply individuals' wants in economically efficient ways. Other institutions that we will examine in the next chapter do likewise in some other circumstances where markets are less effective. But many goods and services are collective in nature. Leaving payment for them to individual decision generally fails. Each person will usually aim to minimize his or her contribution towards the cost of a good or service, hoping to get a free ride on the contributions of others. When too many people try this, the total contributions fail to cover the cost and the good or service cannot be provided. This is a bad equilibrium of a prisoners' dilemma game: not contributing is privately the best strategy for each person regardless of what others are doing, but when they all do this, the result is bad for them all.

It doesn't suffice to educate people about the dilemma and ask them to be less selfish. True, if people were sufficiently other-regarding, they would not try free riding. But despite the finding of behavioural economics that people are not totally selfish, the degree of altruism observed is generally too low to achieve adequate provision of most collective goods and services on a purely voluntary basis in economies involving millions of people. Remember Yossarian in *Catch 22*, who did not want to be among the last to die in a war that was almost won. When his superior officer argued 'But suppose everyone felt that way', he replied 'Then I'd certainly be a damned fool to feel any other way, wouldn't I?'

Collective action to resolve such dilemmas is one reason why, as the preamble to the 1776 American declaration of independence says, 'governments are instituted among men, deriving their just powers from the consent of the governed'. The government can levy taxes or other charges to finance the provision of collective goods and services.

I say 'can' deliberately, because provision by the government using taxes may not be the only or even the best method of supplying many collective goods. We must distinguish two aspects of such a good. One is its collective nature: it can be consumed or used simultaneously by several people, unlike say a slice of bread: when one person eats that, no one else can then consume it. The other is the impossibility of excluding non-payers from consuming or benefiting from the good or service. National defence may be the ultimate example: when a country is attacked, the military defends all citizens; those who have failed to pay their taxes cannot be selectively offered to the enemy to be captured or killed! Collectively consumed and non-excludable goods and services are called *pure public goods*.

In reality, collective consumption and exclusion are both matters of degree. A road can accommodate many drivers, but gets congested and therefore available at a lower quality if too many drivers arrive simultaneously. Exclusion may be possible to a sufficient degree to allow a private entity to finance provision of many collective goods. Even lighthouses, seemingly available for free to all ships passing by, could be and were financed from fees charged to ships using nearby harbours. Toll roads have existed for centuries. Gated communities hire private guards to protect residents. Services with widespread public benefit like education, health care, and rubbish collection can be privately produced even if they are paid out of taxes, and often that works better than public production. With all these qualifications, the government does have a role in provision of goods and services that come close to the conceptual category of pure public goods.

Political economy of policy

We have seen several reasons why markets fail to deliver the magic their most fervent believers expect. The main categories of market failures are monopoly power, externalities, collective goods, and costs of asymmetric information. In each case, a government can design and implement policies to improve market outcomes or sometimes even replace markets altogether. In fact an opposing group of fervent believers expects miracles from governments. In my judgement matters are more subtle and complex. Governments have their own failures, distinct from failures of markets. Judicious selection would let each institution operate in domains where it delivers better outcomes, but there is no reliable mechanism for such selection either. In practice societies must muddle through, accepting some inefficiencies but hoping to detect and correct them before they become too severe.

Why do many people believe in the magic of markets? Usually because they mistakenly believe that the outcome will always be (Pareto) efficient, without any of the qualifications and limitations that I have stressed. Why do extremists on the other side believe in the magic of governments? Usually because they picture themselves as benevolent planners who can order everything in the economy for the best according to their own criteria of efficiency, equity, fairness, sustainability.... This picture is far from the reality of the process of making and implementing economic policy. The actual process falls short of the ideal in many respects. Here I outline just a few prominent issues.

Even in the best of circumstances, namely a democracy where everyone's vote counts equally, political science tells us that policy outcomes will represent the preferences of the median voter—one who ranks exactly at the fiftieth percentile in the political spectrum in the relevant dimension, for example left to right, or rich to poor. This may or may not reflect the sum of everyone's well-being, let alone concerns like fairness or sustainability.

In fact the process differs from an idealized representative democracy. Access to legislators and officials, voice in the media and public forums, lobbying and political contributions, and in some situations outright bribery, all vital parts of the process of making and implementing policy, are unequally available. The rich have an obvious advantage; so do the organized. For a group with common interests, organizing for political participation is a collective action problem. Contributing money, time, and effort are all matters in which each individual may hope to free ride on others in the group. Different groups succeed in solving this collective action problem to different degrees. As a broad generalization, groups that are relatively small in size, and involve large stakes per member, are better organized than large groups with diffuse interests. US sugar import and price support policies give a dramatic example. These policies keep sugar prices high in the US, benefiting domestic sugar farmers and producers of sugar-substitutes like high-fructose corn syrup (HFCS). It has been estimated that in the mid-1980s the consumers' loss was about $3.9 billion and the producers' gain $2.8 billion, so the net loss to the US economy was $1.1 billion. But with a population of about 250 million at that time, the loss to each consumer was only about $15, not worth agitating or organizing over. The gain to sugar-beet farmers averaged $50,000 each, and the gain to sugarcane farmers averaged $500,000 each! Therefore they organized and lobbied in favour of the restrictive policies.

Individuals, firms, or groups with privileged access to the political arena lobby for policies that favour them at the expense of the citizenry as a whole. Firms and industries benefit by restricting competition, so they can keep prices high and enjoy the profits of monopoly or oligopoly. They want regulation and licensing that deter new domestic firms, and tariffs, quotas, or other barriers to imports. In the latter they are supported by organized labour. Such policies are often said to be pro-business, but that usually means that they favour existing businesses. They discriminate against new entrants who would bring in new ideas, products, and methods, creating competition to incumbents. What benefits the country as a whole is not *pro-business* policy, but *pro-market* policy. That means fostering competition, which brings cost-saving and product-improving innovation, and leads to efficient outcomes.

Any scarcity creates a gain, called *economic rent*, to the scarce item. Figure 18 shows a market where at the price corresponding to the point N the supply would be at the point D corresponding to quantity X. If policy restricts the quantity supplied to X,

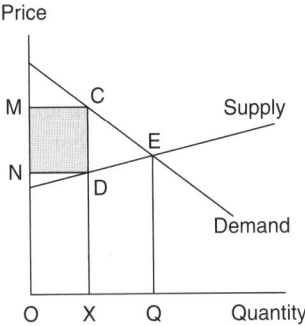

18. Economic rent

demand and supply are equated at C with price M higher than N. Therefore the height MN is the extra gain to each unit of quantity from O to X, and MN times OX, or the area of the shaded rectangle MNDC in the figure, is the total gain or economic rent from the scarcity. Producers of this commodity stand to benefit by creating such scarcity and reaping the rent. If they cannot coordinate to organize the industry as a monopoly or oligopoly, they can lobby the government to institute a scarcity-creating policy under some pretext. Such rent-seeking political activities are common, indeed ubiquitous, and despite the supposedly beneficial motives of the policy sought, are usually detrimental to the interests of the economy as a whole just as private monopolies would be. Barriers against imports are of this kind. So are some certification requirements that restrict entries into professions, limits on the numbers of taxicabs that can operate in a city or the number of restaurants that can serve alcoholic beverages with meals. Existing professionals, cab owners, and restaurateurs benefit at the expense of potential newcomers and the general public.

Effects of bad policies are compounded by the fact that they create special interests that then fight for their continuation. For example the US sugar import restrictions were what made it profitable to produce sugar-substitutes like HFCS. Corn farmers and HFCS firms then became a powerful lobby for preservation of the import restrictions, hurting US consumers economically, and perhaps even in matters of health if claims about the especially unhealthy nature of HFCS are true. The bureaucracies and agencies that implement policies are also a powerful interest resisting policy reforms.

Lobbying and rent-seeking activities are most visible in democracies. That may lead some readers to think that authoritarian or dictatorial regimes would be better for economic efficiencies. Such thinking would also fit with a tendency to think that authoritarian regimes are better for economic development because they are more decisive. For example, many commentators have observed how India's democratic processes slow down the rate of infrastructure construction, and how China proceeds faster by stifling opposition to land acquisition, etc. But authoritarian regimes have their own internal politics and inefficient policies that favour some special groups, often the rulers and their kin, or their ethnic or regional people. Here is the stark and blunt question. Suppose you are convinced of the merits of decisiveness and would like to get an authoritarian ruler for your country. Can you ensure that he or she will turn out to be a Lee Kuan Yew, who brought prosperity to Singapore, and not a Mobutu Sese Seko, who impoverished the Congo?

The financial crisis

The financial crisis started in 2007–8 with a drop in house prices in the US and in many other countries, leading to defaults on home mortgages, and threatened or actual bankruptcies of the financial firms that held these mortgages or mortgage-backed securities. The crisis led to what has come to be called the Great Recession; its effects arguably still persist, despite some recovery in some countries in 2013 at the time of this writing.

This might not appear to be a topic for microeconomics. Its main manifestations, namely high unemployment and a large drop in the gross domestic product (GDP) in many countries, are indeed macroeconomic. But these phenomena were driven by microeconomics—multiple market failures and policy failures of the kind discussed in this chapter. Phil Angelides, chair of the US Financial Crisis Inquiry Commission that met in 2010, hit the nail on the head when he compared the crisis to Agatha Christie's novel *Murder on the Orient Express*, where 'everybody did it'—bankers were greedy, homeowners were gullible, policy-makers pandered to special interests, and so on. I can only touch on a few aspects in this brief account, and have chosen those that provide good examples of market failures and policy failures.

Most financial firms are *intermediaries*: they channel funds between parties that have a surplus of saving or profit (call them 'depositors'), and parties that have a deficit because of needs of spending or investment (call them 'borrowers'). When borrowers promise a higher return on the money they receive than depositors require for the money they supply, the intermediary can carry out a transaction that benefits everyone. It makes a profit for itself while giving each of the two parties the return they offer or require. Of course these activities entail many forms of risks.

First and foremost, the borrower may not deliver the promised return, and in the event of bankruptcy may return nothing, not even the principal. Random shocks such as price fluctuations, natural disasters, and political shifts may destroy the firm's value. But the borrower's incompetence, negligence, or outright fraud may also play a part. The intermediary should develop the skill to judge the borrower's quality, and should exercise due diligence over the borrower's actions. Indeed this is one of the justifications for the existence of the intermediary. The intermediary may also reduce the depositors' risk by lending to several different borrowers with uncorrelated risks. None of these can eliminate the risk entirely.

Second, many financial intermediaries perform *maturity transformation*. This enables depositors to reclaim their money at short or zero notice, which individual borrowers are often unable or unwilling to deliver. Each intermediary deals with many depositors, and only a small fraction of them are likely to want their money back at the same time unless something panics the depositors en masse. Therefore the intermediary is able to hold a relatively small fraction of the deposits as liquid assets or capital reserves, lending the rest at higher returns for longer terms. However, there remains some *liquidity risk* that the intermediary cannot meet the immediate redemption demands of depositors even though it may eventually be able to deliver a high enough return—in other words, it remains *solvent*.

An added complication comes from the fact that depositors' perceptions of liquidity or solvency depend on their beliefs, which may be driven by factors other than the objective circumstances of borrowers or the intermediary. The best example comes from fiction. In *Mary Poppins*, Jane and Michael's father works in a bank. The children are visiting him there, and Michael is carrying two pence to buy food for the birds in Trafalgar Square which they are to visit later that day. Their father's boss wants Michael to deposit the money in the bank, where it will grow. He snatches the two pence from Michael's hand, and Michael shouts 'Give me back my money!' A lady at one of the counters hears him and thinks the bank is running out of money. She asks to withdraw all of her own account at once. Others hear her and do likewise, and there is a run on the bank.

The story shows how liquidity risk can create two equilibria in banking. In one, people believe the bank to be safe. Therefore they are willing to leave their money there, the calls for immediate redemption are low, and the bank is indeed safe. In the other, people doubt the safety of the bank and each tries to get his or her money out at once before it is too late, so the bank fails. The outcome can tip from the former to the latter in response to accidental and mistaken fears, as in the episode from *Mary Poppins*, or to real fears, as when house prices fall and a bank is known to have a large portfolio of mortgages—but real fears get magnified by the process of spreading panic.

Bad loans may create solvency risks for banks, not just liquidity risks. Any carelessness, negligence, or fraud by the borrower raises the risk to the bank and in turn to its depositors. Any carelessness or negligence by the bank in its lending adds to this risk. If all parties had full information about borrowers' or banks' quality and actions, they could enter into a contract with appropriate conditional clauses. For example, depositors could stipulate that the bank should exercise optimal vigilance in its choice of borrowers. But that is clearly unrealistic; information is very asymmetric. Then a bank's carelessness in choosing or monitoring borrowers creates costly risks to depositors, and borrowers' incompetence or negligence creates costly risks to the bank and in turn to its depositors. These are spillovers or externalities caused by information asymmetries. They can be mitigated by vigilance following the dictum 'know your counterparty'. But there are limits to that. Moreover, risks of default can spread in a chain; if A fails to pay what he owes to B, then B may be unable to pay what he owes to C, and so on. Therefore the dictum must be expanded: 'know your counterparty's counterparty; know your counterparty's counterparty's counterparty; and so on'. This is of course impractical. Therefore one bank's actions may create costly risks to other banks and their depositors: information asymmetries can spread and create widespread spillovers. The financial crisis provides many examples.

Home mortgage lending to people with inadequate incomes was perhaps the starting point and driving force of the crisis. Lending decisions were made by bank officers and mortgage brokers who did not expect any penalties if their loans went sour: that would not happen for years, or ever, if commonly held expectations were valid that house prices would never fall. The increase in prices would cover the high future mortgage interest. So the lenders did not care about adverse selection, namely the low quality (low incomes and other indebtedness) of the borrowers. Many homeowners were happy to take these loans in the belief that house prices would rise for ever; many used their homes as cash cows to buy luxury cars, plasma TVs, and other consumer goods that were of low value to banks if repossessed. Governments wanted to extend home-ownership to lower income citizens; therefore regulators overlooked and even encouraged these risky 'subprime' loans. The mortgages were packaged into securities that were rated highly by credit-rating agencies, whose incentives should have been suspect because they were paid by the very firms whose products they were evaluating.

Incentives of intermediaries to exert due diligence in selecting high-quality securities and monitoring them were also lacking. No single depositor had the ability to hold the intermediary to account for lack of diligence. Depositors would have to act collectively, which is difficult. In the case of bank deposits with explicit or implicit government insurance, depositors have no reason to worry about the banks' care in investing their money. In fact they do better when the bank takes big risks: if the risks pay off, they get high returns; if the risks go sour, deposit insurance kicks in and taxpayers bear the loss (as long as the government's full faith and credit is not in doubt). Bank executives likewise prefer risk: they do well if their loans go well and get government bailouts if they go badly. Thus the whole chain of asset holding and transformation was replete with moral hazard and adverse selection poorly controlled by incentives, and made worse by government policies.

The risk inherent in financial intermediation was amplified when retail or commercial banks also engaged heavily in investment banking, and all types of intermediaries traded on their own account, often using debt to leverage their investments. If you use $1 of your own equity and $9 of borrowed money to make a $10 investment, then a mere 10 per cent drop in the value of that investment makes you insolvent. Some banks and other intermediaries such as hedge funds had debt/equity ratios as high as 50.

These risks spread along the whole chain of counterparties. And one failure shakes the public's belief in the soundness of other institutions. Thus externalities arise not only through the direct channel of insolvency, but also through a general loss of faith in, or reputation of, all related financial institutions. For example, when Bear Sterns, an investment bank, was bailed out in March 2008, market speculation against Lehman Brothers increased; when the latter failed in September 2008, the soundness of Merrill Lynch came into question.

The financial crisis quickly spread into an economic crisis. Banks facing risks to their liquidity or solvency cut back on their lending. Firms unable to borrow or even get lines of credit were unable to expand or even sustain employment. The loss of income led to lower demand in the economy, and in turn to lower production and employment. Monetary easing and fiscal stimulus had to be used on an unprecedented scale to prop up demand and prevent the whole economic machinery grinding to a halt for lack of the lubrication that finance provides. Thus microeconomics of the financial sector—bad incentives and externalities—was the root cause of the macroeconomic effects—loss of output and high unemployment.

Financial institutions claim that regulation is unnecessary and even harmful. This could be just a blind and misplaced faith in the magic of the market. On a more generous interpretation, the assertion is they can govern themselves, handling the externalities by Coasian methods. These claims were strongly supported by

Alan Greenspan when he was Chairman of the US Federal Reserve Board, and accepted by successive presidents. Few outsiders hold this belief after the financial crisis. The need for some form of regulation is widely accepted, although the design of the best form of regulation is a matter for debate, and different countries have taken different approaches. Most involve some constraint on debt and risk-taking by retail banks. At one time the Glass-Steagall Act in the US imposed total separation of retail and investment banking. Few support a return to that now, but some separation—installing 'firewalls' or 'ring-fencing' riskier investment banking activities—is often recommended, for example by the UK Independent Commission on Banking. Other proposals include 'macroprudential regulation', which consists mainly of Pigovian measures to control externalities inflicted by the excessive risk-taking of one intermediary on others. Such measures include requiring certain minimum ratios of equity capital or liquid reserves by banks, or other forms of taxing debt and leverage. Regulators can also establish procedures for orderly resolution of insolvencies that are bound to occur from time to time because of risks inherent in investments; this can minimize the risk of failure spreading along a chain of counterparties. Almost no one advocates much greater government role, which would probably result in lending governed by political priorities rather than economic merit, and stifle good innovation along with bad.

Most insiders in financial institutions oppose reforms that increase government regulation, perhaps in the belief that they are better off with the status quo: they get to keep risky profits secure in the knowledge that governments will come to their rescue when the risks go bad, so taxpayers bear the losses. I think they are mistaken to resist all regulation. Making themselves subject to effective regulation is a commitment and a signal that they are of good quality and will behave prudently. This will increase the public's confidence, reduce the risk of panics and liquidity crises, and therefore serve the long-term interests of all banks better.

Chapter 6
Institutions and organizations

Humankind has moved farther away from self-sufficiency for thousands of years. Specialization according to comparative advantage, whether based on resource endowments or skill differences, organization of production in large volumes and long runs, and accumulation of capital equipment have all yielded huge increases in productivity. And decreases in transport costs have made it possible to trade the resulting goods and services for the benefit of consumers across the globe.

Each of these developments entails increasing numbers and complexity of transactions among the specialized individuals and firms. These transactions in turn require an infrastructure of institutions and organizations. Markets are the most common and best known of such institutions—that is why they have been the focus of microeconomics and of this book. But other arrangements for transacting do exist, and can be better than markets for some purposes. We saw in Chapter 3 how firms can use internal organization to save on transaction costs of using markets. Families, social groups and networks, industry associations, and governments work better in other contexts. Study of these institutions enriches microeconomics, and builds bridges between it and other social sciences that study these institutions from their own perspectives.

Property rights and contract enforcement

Successful specialization and transaction have two basic prerequisites—security of property and of contract. If property is insecure, people will not improve land, undertake research and development, accumulate capital, or do any of the things that are so important for increasing the productive potential of the economy, for fear that the fruits of their labours and saving will be stolen. Insecurity of contract will jeopardize all transactions except a few trivial ones where one good or service of perfectly known quality is being exchanged for another equally sure good or service or for cash. All but the most primitive economies need institutions to protect property and enforce contracts.

Although security of property and contract is important, I must invoke my mantra in this context too: nothing is 100 per cent secure. The best of democracies take away private property for public purposes under the legal doctrine of 'eminent domain'. This should be rare, the laws and procedures that allow it to happen should be clear and open, and the owners should be given fair compensation. Contracts are not sacrosanct either; under exceptional circumstances beyond control of the parties to a contract, for example in the case of wars, riots, hurricanes, and earthquakes, one or both parties are freed from their contractual obligations and liabilities. Bankruptcy of a party also frees it from contracts; others dealing with it must take their place in the queue of claimants to whatever can be salvaged. Of course powers of eminent domain are sometimes misused, or the compensation is inadequate, and some companies use the threat of bankruptcy to elicit wage contract concessions from their workers. But most modern economies have enough security of property and contract to be able to support high levels of economic activities and transactions.

State and non-state institutions of governance

Most modern economies rely on the state's laws, and the organizations (police and courts) that enforce the laws, to provide the needed security of property and contract. But in many countries, and in all countries at some time in history, the state's institutions and organizations are or have been too weak, slow, inefficient, biased, or corrupt to be reliable. Such societies develop alternative institutions to provide the needed economic governance. Even in modern advanced economies, non-state institutions supplement state ones, and are superior for some purposes.

All voluntary economic transactions promise gain to both parties; otherwise one or the other would have refused the deal in the first place. But one or both can gain by violating the terms of the contract and behaving opportunistically at the expense of the other party. This is a prisoners' dilemma that needs some resolution, and a contract enforcement institution can provide that. Diego Gambetta studied one such non-state institution in his book on the Sicilian mafia. He quotes a cattle breeder he interviewed: 'When the butcher comes to me to buy an animal, he knows that I want to cheat him [by giving him a low-quality animal]. But I know that he wants to cheat me [by reneging on payment]. [W]e need Peppe [the Mafioso] to make us agree. And we both pay Peppe a percentage of the deal.' I will return to Peppe's enforcement methods, for now leaving you in suspense!

The long arm of the law, or the strong arm of the Mafia, is least needed for repeated transactions between family members and close friends. They can resolve their prisoners' dilemmas in favour exchanges because each values continuation of the relationship more than the short-term gain he or she would make by behaving opportunistically. In good relationships the parties don't even keep precise track of who owes the other more favours, relying on the needs to even out over time. Trying to keep an exact score can spell the end of the relationship; asking for or offering money is totally unacceptable. A memorable example in a different 'family' context comes from *The Godfather*. When the undertaker Bonasera, who is unused to the ways of that world, asks Don Vito Corleone how much he should pay for the service of avenging his daughter's rape, the Don replies: 'Some day, my friend, and may that day never come, I will call on you to do me some small favour. Until then, please accept this as a gift.'

In some situations, one person may not have sufficiently frequently repeated interaction with the same other person, but has frequent occasions to deal with *someone* from a relatively small community. Among businesspeople in a small city, for example, A may deal with B only rarely, but has to deal with some others, be they C, D, etc., all the time. Such groups can develop systems of norms, communication, and multilateral sanctions to sustain honesty in contracts among their members. The norm has two parts. The first forbids members from opportunistically cheating another member. If anyone violates this norm, the group's communication network informs all members. The sanction is that no one in the group will in future have any dealings with the miscreant. Thus if A cheats B, in future C, D, etc., will not deal with A, effectively putting him or her out of business. The fear of this multilateral punishment keeps A honest. But what if C, D, etc., are tempted by profitable business opportunities with A? Therefore the norm has a second part: refusal to participate in A's punishment is itself a violation, with the same punishment of ostracism. The fear of this keeps C, D, etc., in line.

This is similar to honour codes at several universities. Students are required to abide by specified standards of academic integrity in their studies and exams. If a student sees another student violating the code, he or she must report it to the honour committee. Failure to report is itself a violation of the code, calling forth punishments similar to those for primary violations like cheating or plagiarism.

As usual, such systems don't work perfectly or 100 per cent of the time, but work well enough to have existed in many places at many times. Here are two examples from very different places and times:

Avner Greif describes and analyses a community of Jewish merchants in the Maghrib (nations in the Mediterranean coastal plain of North Africa) in the eleventh century AD. They sent goods to other markets hundreds of miles away, relying on agents there to sell them at a good price and to remit the proceeds. Merchants' agents could be opportunistic in many ways—not possess the business skill they claimed to have in order to get the job; claim that the goods had arrived damaged; not do a diligent search for the best available price; falsely claim that the goods had to be sold for a low price and pocket the difference; and so on. The merchants also exchanged letters among themselves on various business matters, and in these they would voice complaints about agents' misbehaviour. If enough evidence mounted, the community would ostracize the miscreant.

Lisa Bernstein studies an arbitration forum of diamond merchants in New York to resolve contract disputes that might arise between them. The arbitrators are experienced merchants in that industry, so they know the prevailing practices and norms, and can assess evidence better than a court that lacks the industry-specific knowledge. Therefore arbitration works faster, is cheaper, and more accurate. If the party judged to be at fault defies the arbitration panel's ruling (usually restitution or fine), the miscreant's name and picture is displayed on the bulletin board of the Diamond Merchants' Club, warning other members against dealing with him or her. This punishment, being driven from business and essentially losing one's livelihood, is far harsher than the fines a court could levy, and is therefore a more effective deterrent against opportunism. With some other arbitration forums, their rulings are respected and enforced by the state's courts.

In these examples, members of the trading community provided their own services for the mechanism of contract governance. In other instances they hire the services of an outsider. Gambetta's Peppe is one of these. He provides two kinds of services. In one, he gathers and stores information about past behaviour of traders. If A has found a profitable business opportunity with B, he can for a fee ask Peppe to disclose whether B cheated in any of his past dealings with others. (Of course Peppe may conspire with B and give A a false assurance; Peppe's fee has to be large enough that he would not want to ruin his reputation as an honest informant for sake of the one-time gain he could get by colluding with B.) If a previously honest B nonetheless cheats A in this deal, Peppe in this mode takes no action other than adding B's name to the list of cheats for future reference, and future loss of business is the only penalty B faces. In the other mode, Peppe is not concerned with past actions. If A is his client and B cheats A, Peppe will inflict on B some suitable harm—smashing kneecaps or worse. Not surprisingly, Peppe's fee for the kneecap-smashing mode is higher than that for tracking and supplying information about past behaviour.

Antecedents for Peppe in the information mode go back to trade fairs in medieval Europe. Merchants from faraway countries gathered together for these. The law governing their contracts, known as *lex mercatoria* or *law merchant*, evolved as a system of custom and practice, and formed the basis for formal contract laws in many countries. Private judges administered the law; they had expertise acquired from their commercial background and a reputation for fairness and giving speedy, effective justice. They charged a fee for their services, which included supplying information about the parties' past behaviour, adjudicating disputes, and keeping their information up to date for future use by adding names of new cheats and those who failed to abide by their rulings. This institution also has similarities with arbitration in the Diamond Merchants' Club.

Such private institutions for contract enforcement work quite well because they serve communities whose members all benefit from the security of trade that successful governance brings. Private institutions for property right protection are more difficult to sustain, because they must deter non-members who would benefit if the institution failed. Nonetheless, they can work when the stakes are sufficiently large. For example, California's gold rush started in 1849 before the territory became a state and established a formal law enforcement mechanism, but the prospectors organized to create and enforce a system of rights to mines. But creation of private rights to products of federal timber and range lands in the US's far west in the late nineteenth century were less successful because the number of people involved was larger and they had more heterogeneous interests.

Private institutions of economic governance work quite well in relatively small stable communities. But the transaction opportunities available within such communities may be limited. Benefits of specialization, economies of large-scale production, and consumption of a wide variety of goods require dealing with others far away—geographically, socially, and economically. Such arm's length transactions with strangers require better objective institutions of governance. Intermediaries who set up a market or market-like platform can help. Let us look at some institutions of this kind.

Market design

The needs of some specialized transactions are best met by creating special markets or market-like platforms for the two sides in a transaction to meet. Some of these even create limited-purpose monies for their transactions. Babysitters' clubs are a well-known example, but they are confined to groups of friends, or at least acquaintances, in a small geographic area. The internet has greatly expanded the scope of such markets, and has created what is being termed a 'sharing economy' or 'peer-to-peer economy'.

Airbnb created a private market for rentals of rooms, apartments, or houses, matching hosts and guests. Each party has good reason to worry about entering into the transaction with a stranger. The host worries that the guests may be dirty, noisy, or obnoxious, or may even steal from them; the guests worry about the quality of the accommodation. The owners of the platform carry out some background checks; they also invite ratings from previous users. Hosts without previous record must accept low rents—as they accumulate good ratings they can raise their price. Of course the system is not perfect. For example, you could get your friends to give you good ratings. But on the whole the system seems to be working fairly well for Airbnb. Similar sites exist for rentals of private cars, do-it-yourself tools and equipment, and so on.

Other sites such as eBay, Craiglist, the outside vendors on Amazon, and so on cover a broader range of goods and services. To be successful, all markets or trading platforms must pay attention to several matters. They must facilitate searches for counterparties to the trade each individual using the site wants and match the two sides. They must also facilitate price discovery, helping sellers search for the highest price they can get, and buyers search for the lowest price they must pay (with appropriate adjustment for quality, delivery time, etc.). And they must ensure contractual performance and resolve disputes. Traditional marketplaces—central squares in towns, medieval market fairs, modern malls, stock exchanges, and so on—enabled search and matching by bringing together potential traders at one physical site; on the internet the site is geographically scattered across a million computers or other devices but connected electronically. Smartphones have even facilitated price discovery across markets—for example, fishermen off the southwest coast of India can get information about prices in different coastal towns and decide where to take their catch. All these developments promote economic efficiency by making markets more competitive and making it easier to achieve equilibrium of supply and demand. (These transactions usually avoid the taxes that would be levied on sales in the conventional formal economy; it must be admitted that in some cases that is their raison d'etre.) The needs of contract performance and dispute resolution are met by one of various institutions: the state's machinery of law, industry arbitration, reputations based on peer-reviews and ratings, and so on.

Matching markets

Many transactions involve matching people or objects in pairs, and platforms and institutions exist to facilitate such transactions. People seeking marriage partners and informal or formal matchmaking institutions are the most obvious example, but many others exist: applicants and colleges, students and dormitory rooms, newly graduated doctors and hospitals, organ donors and patients who need transplants, and so on. In some contexts matches must meet certain constraints; for example organs and recipients must be of compatible blood types. In other cases each item on one side could be matched with any of several on the other side, but one or both have preferences among the alternatives: college students have preferences about dorm rooms but not vice versa, but colleges and applicants both have preferences about their matches, as do the prospective bride and groom in marriage. It is important to examine whether existing platforms or institutions achieve matches that are good in some suitable sense, and whether better ones can be designed.

Conventional markets would be problematic in many matching situations. First, items are indivisible and heterogeneous, and numbers of items on each side may be small. Markets may turn into bargaining among pairs, where each member of each pair has significant market power. Second, the use of money is sometimes not customary, and may be abhorrent especially in contexts like organ transplants. Money is sometimes used in disguise; for example, colleges offer better financial aid packages to students they wish to attract, and dowry or bride price payments exist in many cultures. But constraints or prohibition on the use of money complicates matching transactions beyond what is usual in markets.

The theory of matching markets was pioneered by David Gale, Lloyd Shapley, and others; it was extended with several important applications including hospital-doctor matching, organ donation being developed by Alvin Roth and others. Shapley and Roth won the 2012 economics Nobel prize for their contributions. (Gale had died in 2008.) Here is my selective and very short introduction to this work.

What are desirable properties of a matching process? First, of course, comes the economists' obsession: Pareto efficiency. It should not be feasible to devise another matching that leaves all participants better off (i.e. with matches higher in their order of preference). A related property is stability. Label the participants on one side with upper-case letters and those on the other side with lower-case letters. Suppose a mechanism matches A with a, and B with b, but A prefers to be matched with b, and b with A. In the absence of coercion, A and b would be able to get together and do better than they would have done in the outcome of the mechanism, which would therefore be unstable. If no such voluntary exits in pairs are possible, the outcome is stable. When participants' preferences are not known to others, as is often the case, a third desirable property is non-manipulability: no participant should be able to get a better outcome by misrepresenting his or her preferences.

When only one side of the market has preferences over its matches, as with college students and dorm rooms, a simple procedure called top-trading cycle can meet these desiderata. Start with any assignment: this could be the status quo or initial ownership pattern. Each student indicates his or her most preferred room. If the initial pairing is unstable, a set of students can each get their top preferences by swapping rooms among themselves. Let them do this, and remove them from the market. Repeat the process with the remaining students with their preferences over the remaining rooms. Continue until all rooms have been allocated. It has been proved that this method has all three properties—stability, Pareto efficiency, and non-manipulability. Of course, as always with Pareto efficiency, the outcome depends on the initial assignment and need not be equal or fair; if you are not lucky enough to be in one of the early rounds of swapping cycles, your top preferences may be gone before you get your turn.

Things get more complex when both sides have preferences over their matches. As an example, consider four students a, b, c, and d applying to four colleges A, B, C, and D. Table 4 shows the preference using > to indicate a higher place in the preference ranking. For example, college B likes student d best, a second, c third, and b last.

The matching procedure devised by Gale and Shapley, called the deferred acceptance algorithm, works as follows. Choose one side, let us say the colleges, to make offers. Each college makes an offer to the student it ranks highest. In our example, A offers to a, B and D offer to d, and C offers to b. Each student holds on to the offer he or she likes best and rejects the others. Here d has two

Table 4. Example of matching with two-sided preferences

Colleges' preferences		Students' preferences	
A	$a > b > d > c$	a	$D > B > A > C$
B	$d > a > c > b$	b	$D > A > B > C$
C	$b > a > d > c$	c	$D > B > C > A$
D	$d > c > b > a$	d	$A > C > B > D$

offers, from B and D, of which she prefers B, so rejects D. Of the others, a and b have one offer each, and hold on to these; c has no offers and waits for the second round. Importantly, acceptances are not binding yet; hence the title 'deferred acceptance'. In the second round, D (which was rejected by d in the first round) offers to its next preference, namely c. Now c has one offer, and accepts it. Each student has an offer, and the procedure stops. The matches A–a, B–d, C–b, and D–c become binding.

What if students are the side that make the offers? In the first round students a, b, and c make offers to college D, and d to A. Now D has three offers, and accepts c (its top preference among them), rejecting a and b. In the second round, a offers to B and b to A. Now A has two offers, from d in the first round and b in the second round, and rejects the less-preferred, namely d. (Remember that acceptances are not binding until the procedure stops.) In the third round, d offers to its next-ranked college, C. Now we have a one-to-one matching, namely a–B, b–A, c–D, and d–C. The matches are finalized, and the procedure stops.

It can be proved that the procedure leads to stable outcomes, and is Pareto efficient for the side that makes the offers. However, it is manipulable: someone from the side that receives the offer can usually achieve a better outcome by strategically misrepresenting his or her preferences. In the above example, when colleges make offers, acting according to true preferences gets student d college B, which ranks third in her preferences. If she pretended to have preferences A > C > D > B, she would get college C, which is second in her true preferences! The reasoning is lengthy and the procedure takes six rounds; suspicious or diligent readers may wish to construct it for a good mental exercise.

Evolution of the programme for matching hospitals with new graduates of medical schools is instructive. In the first half of the twentieth century this was a largely decentralized market. In the 1940s, US hospitals competed for the best medical students by offering them internships earlier and earlier. This did not work well, because matches were fixed before the quality of the students or their interests in particular specializations became clear. And if an offer was rejected, it became too late to make another offer to an acceptable candidate. In the 1950s the National Resident Matching Program started, and worked like the deferred acceptance algorithm where hospitals made offers. It continues, with some changes, notably applicant-proposing instead of hospital-proposing, and accommodating married couples of doctors who seek joint offers.

The procedure can be generalized to allow for the possibility that some matches are worse than no match at all and therefore unacceptable to one side or the other. It can also be generalized to situations where each item on one side is to be matched with several on the other side, as is the case with colleges and students.

Another important platform matches kidney donors and recipients. These often come in pairs where one person is willing to donate a kidney to a relative or loved one who needs one, but has an incompatible blood type. Situations may arise in which A is willing to donate to a and B to b, but the willing pairs are incompatible, whereas A is compatible with b and B with a. This requires a coordinated set of operations in which A and B donate simultaneously, and the organs are transplanted into b and a, respectively. Even more complex chains of many donors and recipients are being coordinated using centralized clearinghouses.

Auctions

Many transactions are conducted as auctions rather than sales at posted or negotiated prices. An auction brings together all potential buyers for the designated commodity (or package of commodities) to create some form of competition among them. In fact that is why many sellers use auctions. Bidding for supply or construction contracts is the mirror-image, where the buyer brings together potential and competing sellers.

Auctions take many different forms. In a sealed-bid auction, each bidder submits a bid without knowing what any of the others are doing. The seller inspects all bids simultaneously. The highest bidder gets the object and pays what he or she has bid. A similar outcome is achieved if the seller starts a 'price clock' at a very high level and gradually lowers it. At any time any of the bidders can stop the clock and claim the object at that price. In the reverse of this process, the seller starts a price clock at a low level and continuously raises it. Bidders can drop out at any time (but cannot then re-enter). When only one bidder remains, he or she gets the object at the price on the clock, which is the price at which the bidder with the second-highest willingness to pay dropped out. In the familiar ascending or 'open outcry' form where the auctioneer asks 'any advance on' the previous bid, or raises bids in increments and bidders can stay in or drop out, the one willing to pay the most is the last survivor, but pays only a little more than the second-highest willingness to pay. (I said 'a little more' because bids may jump discretely in this form. Suppose A has the highest willingness to pay, offering \$120, and B is next at \$112. The auctioneer ups the bids in increments of \$5. Both bidders are in at \$110. B drops out at \$115. A is willing to pay \$120 but pays only \$115, 'a little more' than \$112. With a continuously rising clock, B would drop out as soon as the clock crossed \$112, and A would pay that; okay, \$112.01 perhaps.) This is explicit in a *second-price auction*, where the rules state directly that the highest bidder wins but pays only the second-highest bid. By contrast, the form where the highest bidder wins and pays his or her own bid is called a *first-price auction*.

There even are 'all pay' auctions where the highest bidder gets the object, but all bidders, win or lose, pay whatever they had bid. You may think this very odd, but this is perhaps the commonest form in everyday life. In every four-year cycle for election to the US presidency, numerous politicians spend huge amounts of time, effort, and money; these expenditures are like bids. Only one succeeds every four years, and the losers don't get any refunds on their bids. The same goes for athletes training to win medals at the Olympic games, contestants for lucrative contracts, and so on.

Each bidder formulates a bidding strategy; the seller decides the form of the auction, and perhaps a minimum or 'reserve' price. This makes the auction a game of strategy. It is complicated by asymmetric information. The seller may know things about the object that the bidders don't. Each bidder attaches a value to the object. This may be personal or sentimental (Audrey Hepburn's little black dress in *Breakfast at Tiffany's*) or commercial (an estimate of the amount of crude oil in a tract being auctioned). Any one bidder doesn't know other bidders' value directly, but something may be revealed in the process of bidding, for example how quickly some of the others drop out in an ascending, open outcry auction. The seller does not know the bidders' valuations; if he or she did he or she would simply go to the highest valuer and offer to sell at a price just below that value. The outcome of the auction is an equilibrium of this subtle game of asymmetric information with big practical applications. No wonder research on the topic has burgeoned in economic theory and game theory. I can just begin to touch on a couple of major themes.

In a first-price auction, a bid equal to your valuation of the object will not get you any profit or surplus even if you win. Bidding less than your value decreases your probability of winning, but gets you more profit if you do win. Your bidding strategy should balance these two considerations; the result is that your bid should be somewhat below your value. In a second-price auction, what you pay if you do win is someone else's bid, which is outside your control. Therefore your best strategy is to maximize your probability of winning, namely to make your bid equal to your full valuation. Now look at these strategies from the seller's perspective. If the seller uses a first-price form, bidders will shade their bids below their values; if a second-price form, they will bid their values but the seller will get only the second-highest value. Which earns the seller the higher revenue? In any one instance, the bidders' configuration of values and bids may take the outcome in either direction. But the seller does not know these values in advance. Taking the appropriate probabilistic averages over all configurations, it turns out that under very broad conditions the two effects (underbidding in the first-price form and getting only the second-highest value in the second-price form) exactly cancel out: the two forms are revenue-equivalent! In fact this revenue-equivalence holds for all auction forms under these conditions; this was an amazing early insight of auction theory.

Next consider an auction where the item has an objective or commercial value, but different bidders have different estimates of this value. If their estimation processes are unbiased and there are many bidders (say 100), by the law of large numbers (the wisdom of crowds) the average of their estimates will be close to the true value. But the average bid does not win the auction; the highest bid does. This will be based on the highest estimate of value, which by that very fact is likely to be an overestimate. A truly strategic bidder will recognize this, and think: 'If I win, that means 99 other bidders got lower estimates than I did. What should I learn from that, and how should it affect my bid?' The answer is to shade your bid downward. The mathematics for calculating how much to shade is complex, and in practice many bidders fail to make the correct inferences, with the result that often the winners of rights to mineral and crude oil deposits find that they have paid too much; or sports teams that win the competition for a superstar find that the player does not live up to their expectations. This is known as the *winner's curse*.

Less well-known is a hypothetical phenomenon of a loser's curse. Suppose 99 objects are being auctioned among 100 bidders, and you are the one who loses out. That means you got an exceptionally low estimate of the value. You should have asked yourself: 'If I lose, that means 99 other bidders gave higher estimates than I did. What should I learn from that, and how should it affect my bid?' Here you should raise your bid to correct for the loser's curse.

Now consider a middle range where the ratio of the number of objects to that of bidders is not too lopsided: it is neither too close to 0 (1 object and 100 bidders) nor too close to 1 (99 objects and 100 bidders). Then neither the winner's curse nor the loser's curse has much bite; each bidder can ignore the fact that others have different information and bid based on his or her own valuation. That gives us a really subtle but enlightening way to understand how competitive markets with many buyers and sellers work efficiently, even though the relevant information is widely scattered among all participants. We started out with markets and diverged to consider other platforms and institutions; it is nice to come full circle in closing.

Chapter 7
What works?

If you were hoping for a grand finale, declaring the triumph of the market, or the end of capitalism as we know it, I must disappoint you. In Chapter 4, I showed how competitive markets, when they perform well, yield Pareto efficient outcomes. If you recall the definition: no other feasible outcome can bring greater economic benefit for some people and losses to none. However, a Pareto efficient outcome may have a very unfair distribution of well-being. In Chapter 5, I showed how monopoly, externalities, and information asymmetries can prevent market outcomes from being efficient even in the limited Pareto sense. And, to pile on the bad news, governments often don't deliver any better outcomes. They have their own failures stemming from the nature of political processes, whether democratic or authoritarian. They have their own favourites and clients—existing producers, other organized interests, and campaign contributors—who benefit at the expense of the general public.

Given this long list of defects in markets and governments, the world has fared not too badly. Mixed economies, comprising on the one hand markets and similar institutions that rely on incentives and self-interest, and on the other hand communal institutions and governments to organize collective action, to provide oversight, limit abuses of market power, and deploy taxes or other policies that correct market failures, have achieved reasonable economic outcomes and growth in many countries. I think such muddling through is the most we can hope for.

In my view the biggest risk facing a reasonably good outcome is failure to notice and correct errors before they spiral out of control and do serious damage. This risk is at its worst when one person or one organization controls all pertinent decisions. So long as a competitor can spot the first decision-maker's errors and has a profit or other incentive to correct them, all will be reasonably well. Therefore I am not for or against markets or governments per se, but against monopoly of either kind.

An egregious example of the effects of monopoly over decisions comes from post World War II urban planning and public housing. Influenced by theories of Le Corbusier and others, government agencies designed and built deserts like Brasilia and horrors like the Pruitt-Igoe projects in St Louis. If urban housing had been provided by competitive private builders, at least some of them would have quickly noticed the defects of such developments and offered alternatives. However, government agencies persisted with their plans. Even worse was the horror of McCarthyism in the US, which stigmatized many people with suspicion of treason and barred them from employment in the government and in many, although not all, private firms. Paul Samuelson, surely one of the top five economists of the twentieth century, drew this lesson when describing his life philosophy in a 1983 article in *The American Economist*:

> What I learned from the McCarthy incident was the peril of a one-employer society. When you are blackballed from government employment, there is great safety in the existence of thousands of anonymous employers out there in the market....To me this became a newly perceived argument, not so much for laissez faire capitalism as for the mixed economy.

A mixed economy—where competitive markets or similar institutions generate information about scarcity and create incentives to alleviate the scarcity in a reasonably efficient manner, where antitrust policies keep the markets open to competition, where the government and other social organizations help overcome the inefficiencies of externalities, and where political competition acts as a corrective mechanism against abuses of power and serious errors of judgement—is in my opinion the best way of organizing microeconomic activity.

Further reading

General

In my judgement the best book about markets—how they work, what they accomplish, and why and how they can fail—is *Reinventing the Bazaar* by John McMillan (W. W. Norton, 2002). If you have time to read only one book about economics, make it this one.

At a slightly more technical level, Milton Friedman's *Price Theory*, originally published in 1962 (reprinted in 2001 by Martino Fine Books), is still highly worth reading. I got my own introduction to practically applicable microeconomic theory from it.

Among modern college textbooks, there is an abundance of excellent material. At the risk of doing injustice to numerous others, let me mention two with authors who are my co-authors in other contexts: Robert Pindyck and Daniel Rubinfeld, *Microeconomics* (Prentice-Hall, 7th edition, 2008); and Douglas Bernheim and Michael Whinston, *Microeconomics* (McGraw-Hill/Irwin, 2007).

For historical background, William J. Bernstein's *A Splendid Exchange: How Trade Shaped the World* (Atlantic Monthly Press, 2008) is a sweeping and fascinating tale of world trade and markets through the ages.

Chapter 2: Consumers

The Friedman, Pindyck-Rubinfeld, and Bernheim-Whinston books all analyse conventional consumer choice at an introductory level and in detail far beyond what is possible in this very short introduction. The latter two books also discuss modern behavioural approaches. At an advanced level, in my view the best treatment of the theory and empirics of consumer choice is still Angus Deaton and John Muellbauer's *Economics and Consumer Behavior* (Cambridge University Press, 1980). Readers with good economic and statistical preparation will benefit from reading the survey used in the text: Richard Blundell, 'Consumer Behaviour: Theory and Empirical Evidence—A Survey,' *Economic Journal*, 98(389), March 1988, 16–65.

For behavioural approaches to decision theory, Daniel Kahneman's *Thinking Fast and Slow* (Farrar, Straus and Giroux, 2011) is the best introduction. Richard Thaler's *The Winner's Curse: Paradoxes and Anomalies of Economic Life* (Princeton University Press, 1994) was an early account of the accumulating research that led to changes in economists' thinking. Thaler and Cass Sunstein's *Nudge: Improving Decisions About Health, Wealth, and Happiness* (Penguin Books, 2009) argues the case for, and gives examples of, 'soft paternalism' based on behavioural research. For the application to environmental policies, see Cass R. Sunstein and Lucia A. Reisch, 'Automatically Green: Behavioral Economics and Environmental Protection' (5 April 2013). Available at SSRN: <http://dx.doi.org/10.2139/ssrn.2245657>.

Chapter 3: Producers

More detailed classification and analysis of costs—fixed and variable, average and marginal, sunk and avoidable … and implications for shapes of supply curves can be found in any introductory textbook.

Tim Harford's *The Undercover Economist* (Oxford University Press, 2006, chapters 1 and 2) has an excellent discussion and many examples of screening strategies for price discrimination. It is also great reading for much else about how economics enters our daily lives. Michael Porter's *Competitive Strategy* (Free Press, 1980) is the classic monograph about firms' strategies in competition with rival firms in their industry. Porter himself and many others have written books elaborating, extending, modifying, or challenging its teachings. Interested readers can discover this literature by searching for the book on <http://scholar.google.com>.

Study of strategic competition among firms relies on game theory, which is also useful for elucidating many other political and social strategic interactions. I am biased, but would like to recommend my own (with

Barry Nalebuff) book, *The Art of Strategy* (W. W. Norton 2008) intended for general readership, and my textbook (with Susan Skeath and David Reiley) *Games of Strategy* (W. W. Norton, 3rd edition, 2009). For the fascinating history of the diamond cartel, see Edward Jay Epstein, *The Rise and Fall of Diamonds: The Shattering of a Brilliant Illusion* (Simon and Schuster, 1982). See Austin Ramzy, 'Precious Holdings', *Time*, 18 February 2013, for an account of China's attempt to monopolize the market for rare earth metals, and Paul Klemperer, 'What Really Matters in Auction Design', *Journal of Economic Perspectives*, 16(1), January 2002, 169–89, for a discussion of collusion among bidders in auctions.

The mathematics of screening by self-selection is one of the most subtle and beautiful topics in economic theory. If you are really good at maths—and I mean, *really*: integral calculus and all that—I strongly recommend two articles both of which figured in economics Nobel prizes: James Mirrlees, 'An Exploration in the Theory of Optimal Income Taxation,' *Review of Economic Studies*, 38(2), April 1971, 175–208; and David Baron and Roger Myerson, 'Regulating a Monopolist with Unknown Cost', *Econometrica*, 50(4), July 1982, 911–30.

For detailed statements of the contributions of Ronald Coase and Oliver Williamson that led to a major change in the way economists think about firms, see the Nobel prize web sites: <http://www.nobelprize.org/nobel_prizes/economics/laureates/1991/press.html> and <http://www.nobelprize.org/nobel_prizes/economics/laureates/2009/advanced.html>.

Chapter 4: Markets

My list for this chapter must begin by reiterating a strong recommendation for John McMillan's *Reinventing the Bazaar*. The Bernheim-Whinston and Pindyck-Rubinfeld textbooks cited above offer good detailed and balanced treatments.

Insightful but one-sided accounts include Milton and Rose Friedman, *Free to Choose* (Mariner Books, 1990); and Joseph Stiglitz, *Whither Socialism* (MIT Press, 1996). For the Friedmans, markets are always wonderful and governments should keep away; for Stiglitz, markets, and often even market-based policies, are highly likely to fail and government is the answer.

A classic early analysis of rent controls is Milton Friedman and George Stigler's *Roofs or Ceilings? The Current Housing Problem* (Foundation for Economic Education, 1946).

On market instability, for me the best book is still Charles Kindleberger's *Manias, Panics, and Crashes: A History of Financial Crises* (Basic Books, 1978). Later editions are coauthored with Robert Z. Aliber (Palgrave Macmillan, 2011).

Chapter 5: Market and policy failures

Here I recommend three original books by Nobel laureates that can be read by non-specialists. Ronald Coase's *The Firm, the Market and the Law* (University of Chicago Press, 1995) includes his article on privately negotiated solutions to externalities, as well as his articles on the firm that were mentioned in Chapter 3. Elinor Ostrom's *Governing the Commons: The Evolution of Institutions for Collective Action* (Cambridge University Press, 1990) contains her work on bottom–up management of common pool resources. Remarkably for economics books, these two have no maths at all.

A classic example of Coasian resolutions of externalities is in Steven N. S. Cheung, 'The Fable of the Bees: An Economic Investigation', *Journal of Law and Economics*, 16(1), April 1973, 11–34.

Daniel Spulber has edited a valuable and fascinating collection of articles debunking many popular conceptions about market failures and need for government intervention in *Famous Fables of Economics: Myths of Market Failures* (Wiley-Blackwell, 2001).

Key early chapters of Michael Spence's pathbreaking book, *Market Signaling: Informational Transfer in Hiring and Related Screening Processes* (Harvard University Press, 1974) are highly readable, requiring minimal numeracy. Diego Gambetta's *Codes of the Underworld: How Criminals Communicate* (Princeton University Press, 2011) has many fascinating examples of signalling and screening in organized crime. John Maynard-Smith and David Harper give an excellent overview of biological signaling in their book *Animal Signals* (Oxford University Press, 2004).

Mancur Olson's *The Logic of Collective Action* (Harvard University Press, 1965) and *The Rise and Decline of Nations* (Yale University Press, 1984) are important and readable analyses of how collective action can work or fail in private arrangements, of the importance of concentrated versus diffuse benefits, of how special interests can stifle policy reform that would benefit the economy as a whole and how their power can be broken in a crisis. For an analysis of the political process of economic policymaking, see Avinash Dixit, *The Making of Economic Policy: A Transaction Cost Politics Perspective* (MIT Press, 1996).

In the 1950s and 1960s, Richard Musgrave was influential in establishing the view of government as correcting market failures, and James Buchanan was equally influential in establishing a contrary view of politicians as pursuers of their self-interest rather than larger interests of the country, thereby creating government failures. Therefore it is fascinating to read these two giants in the late years of their lives discuss and debate their opposing views in James M. Buchanan and Richard A. Musgrave, *Public Finance and Public Choice: Two Contrasting Visions of the State* (MIT Press, 1999).

For a general discussion of the economic efficiency costs of monopoly power, see pp. 67–8 of Jean Tirole, *Industrial Organization* (MIT Press, 1991). For the specific example of health care costs in the US, see Steven Brill, 'Bitter Pill: How Outrageous Pricing and Egregious Profits are Destroying our Health Care', *Time*, 4 March 2013. Stephen V. Marks, 'A Reassessment of Empirical Evidence on the U.S. Sugar Program', in *The Economics and Politics of World Sugar Policies*, ed. Steven V. Marks and Keith E. Maskus (University of Michigan Press, 1993), calculates the costs of US sugar import restrictions.

Many instances of policy failure would be outright funny if they were not so costly. My favourite is the Greek ban on banana imports during the 1970s; see Barry Newman, 'The Greeks have a Word for Banana but Lack Bananas', *Wall Street Journal*, July 1983. A Japanese trade official justified their restriction on beef imports by arguing that the Japanese have longer intestines and cannot digest more beef (*New York Times*, 6 March 1988). And France prevented the US multinational Pepsi from acquiring Danone, which makes yogurt and bottled water, on the grounds that it was a national business champion in a strategic industry (*The Telegraph*, 24 July 2005). The US political process of tax reform is brilliantly recounted by Jeffrey H. Birnbaum and Alan S. Murray in *Showdown at Gucci Gulch* (Random House, 1987).

One of the earliest and most perceptive accounts of the financial crisis came in the form of comedy sketches by John Bird and John Fortune on the British television programme, *The South Bank Show*. Some of these are on YouTube; search for 'Bird' and 'Fortune'. Early and perceptive books on the recent financial crisis I recommend are Gillian Tett, *Fool's Gold: How the Bold Dream of a Small Tribe at J. P. Morgan Was Corrupted by Wall Street Greed and Unleashed a Catastrophe* (Free Press, 2010), and Robert Shiller, *The Subprime Solution: How Today's Global Financial Crisis Happened, and What to Do about It* (Princeton University Press, 2009). Among more recent books, Raghuram Rajan, *Fault Lines: How Hidden Fractures Still Threaten the World Economy* (Princeton University Press, 2011) is my favourite. Carmen M. Reinhart and Kenneth S. Rogoff, *This Time Is Different: Eight Centuries of Financial Folly* (Princeton University Press, 2009) is an outstanding study of financial crises through history. Issues of reform are nicely discussed by John Vickers, who chaired the UK Independent Commission on Banking, in 'Some Economics of Banking Reform', Oxford University, Department of Economics, Discussion Paper No. 632, November 2012, available from <http://www.economics.ox.ac.uk/index.php/research/working-papers>.

Chapter 6: Institutions and organizations

For more detailed explanations of the reasons for, and benefits from, specialization in production, see the chapters on trade and growth in any introductory economics textbook, such as Paul Krugman and Robin Wells, *Microeconomics* (Worth Publishers, 3rd edition, 2012, chapter 8). The chapter on growth in their *Macroeconomics* (Worth Publishers, 3rd edition, 2012, chapter 8) is also relevant.

Douglass North's work, exposited in his book *Institutions, Institutional Change, and Economic Performance* (Cambridge University Press, 1990), was important in reviving economists' interest in institutions for property rights and contracts. Oliver E. Williamson started his analysis of firms and broadened it to economic governance more generally; his books *The Economic Institutions of Capitalism* (Free Press, 1987) and *The Mechanisms of Governance* (Oxford University Press, 1996) have been hugely influential. Both of these people won Nobel prizes for their research.

Non-state institutions for property-right protection are studied by Yoram Barzel, *Economic Analysis of Property Rights* (Cambridge University Press, 1989), and Gary D. Libecap, *Contracting for Property Rights* (Cambridge University Press, 1989).

Diego Gambetta, *The Sicilian Mafia: The Business of Private Protection* (Harvard University Press, 1993), is an outstanding ethnographic study of a non-state institution for contract enforcement.

Avner Greif's historical research and game-theoretic modelling of contract enforcement by formal and informal institutions, collected in his book *Institutions and the Path to the Modern Economy: Lessons from Medieval Trade* (Cambridge University Press, 2006) is highly readable. And, if I may be so bold, chapters 1 and 6, and the introductory sections in chapters 2–5 of Avinash Dixit, *Lawlessness and Economics: Alternative Modes of Governance* (Princeton University Press, 2004) are also readable.

A good account of the theory and applications of matching markets is in the advanced information document on the Shapley-Roth Nobel prize: <http://www.nobelprize.org/nobel_prizes/economic-sciences/laureates/2012/advanced.html>.

On auctions, I recommend Paul Klemperer's *Auctions: Theory and Practice* (Princeton University Press, 2004); and Paul Milgrom's *Putting Auction Theory to Work* (Cambridge University Press, 2004). Beginning readers should confine themselves to the introductory chapters.

Peer-to-peer markets are evolving very fast and any description and analysis may get out of date very quickly. But *What's Mine Is Yours: The Rise of Collaborative Consumption* by Rachel Botsman and Roo Rogers (Harper Business Books, 2010) is worth reading.

The concluding point about markets is based on Wolfgang Pesendorfer and Jeroen Swinkels, 'Efficiency and Information Aggregation in Auctions', *American Economic Review*, 90(3), June 2000, 499–525. This is highly mathematical.

Index

Microeconomics

JOIN OUR COMMUNITY

www.oup.com/vsi

- Join us online at the official Very Short Introductions **Facebook** page.
- Access the thoughts and musings of our authors with our online **blog**.
- Sign up for our monthly **e-newsletter** to receive information on all new titles publishing that month.
- Browse the full range of Very Short Introductions online.
- Read **extracts** from the Introductions for free.
- Visit our library of **Reading Guides**. These guides, written by our expert authors will help you to question again, why you think what you think.
- If you are a teacher or lecturer you can order inspection copies quickly and simply via our website.

Visit the Very Short Introductions website to access all this and more for free.

www.oup.com/vsi

ONLINE CATALOGUE
A Very Short Introduction

Our online catalogue is designed to make it easy to find your ideal Very Short Introduction. View the entire collection by subject area, watch author videos, read sample chapters, and download reading guides.

http://fds.oup.com/www.oup.co.uk/general/vsi/index.html

ECONOMICS
A Very Short Introduction
Partha Dasgupta

Economics has the capacity to offer us deep insights into some of the most formidable problems of life, and offer solutions to them too. Combining a global approach with examples from everyday life, Partha Dasgupta describes the lives of two children who live very different lives in different parts of the world: in the Mid-West USA and in Ethiopia. He compares the obstacles facing them, and the processes that shape their lives, their families, and their futures. He shows how economics uncovers these processes, finds explanations for them, and how it forms policies and solutions.

'An excellent introduction . . . presents mathematical and statistical findings in straightforward prose.'

Financial Times

www.oup.com/vsi